BUILDING STRATEGIES

STRATEGIES 2

AN INTEGRATED LANGUAGE COURSE FOR LEARNERS OF ENGLISH

Brian Abbs
Ingrid Freebairn

Longman

Contents

Unit 1   A new start

Set 1 People

1. What's your name?
   Where were you born?
   What nationality are you?
   Where do you live?
   What do you do?
   Where do you work/study?

Work in pairs. Ask your partner in the same way.

2. What's his/her name?   His/her name's....
   Where was he/she born?   He/she was born in....
   What nationality is he/she?   He/she's....
   Where does he/she live?   He/she lives in....
       At the moment he/she is living in....
   What does he/she do?   He/she's a/an....
   Where does he/she work?   He/she works for/in a.... in....
   Where does he/she study?   He/she studies at....

Work in groups. Ask and answer about each other in the same way.

3.

Rod Nelson is a 26-year-old electrical engineer from Ottawa in Canada. He is working in England for a British company called Western Aeronautics. The company is based in Bristol. At the moment Rod is living in a company hostel.

Barbara Cooper is 24 and comes from Bristol. She is the manageress of a shoe shop called 'Pretty Feet' in the centre of Bristol. She has a flat of her own in an old part of the city.

Copy the chart below into your notebooks. Ask and answer questions to complete the chart for either Rod or Barbara.

Name	
Age	
Nationality	
Country of birth	
Country of residence (if different)	
Occupation	

4. Use the notes below to write complete paragraphs about the people.

JACK AND PEGGY COOPER
— about 50
— from Bristol
— Jack = production manager
  at Western Aeronautics
— Peggy = cashier at a
  supermarket called Tesco's
— one daughter, Barbara
— small house on a new estate

JOAN AND NORMAN INGRAMS
— about 35, both born in
  New Zealand
— Joan = part-time secretary
  Norman = accountant
— two children, Mark, 4 and
  Mandy, 6
— large, three-storey house
  in a suburb of Bristol

PAUL BLAKE
— 21
— Welsh (from Cardiff)
— maths, naval engineering
  at Bristol Polytechnic
— student hostel

**5. Write similar paragraphs about yourself and an older relative
   or friend.**

🔲 Open dialogue

Rod Nelson is in the buffet bar at Paddington Station, one of London's main
railway stations. He is waiting for the train to Bristol. He looks for
somewhere to sit down. Use these responses to complete the dialogue:

From Dubrovnik / Goodbye / Mine's Zlatko. Zlatko Tiric / Yes, it is /
No I'm not. I'm Yugoslavian / No, thanks / No, I'm not. I study in London

ROD: Excuse me, is this seat free?
ZLATKO:..........
ROD: You aren't English, are you?
ZLATKO:..........
ROD: Where do you come from in Yugoslavia?
ZLATKO:..........
ROD: Are you here on holiday?
ZLATKO:..........
ROD: My name's Rod, by the way. What's yours?
ZLATKO:..........
ROD: Would you like another coffee?
ZLATKO:..........
ROD: My train leaves in five minutes. I must go.
        Nice meeting you. Bye!
ZLATKO:..........

Now listen to the dialogue and read it in pairs.

Roleplay

This time *you* are the person who meets Rod. In pairs,
read the dialogue again.

Set 2 Places

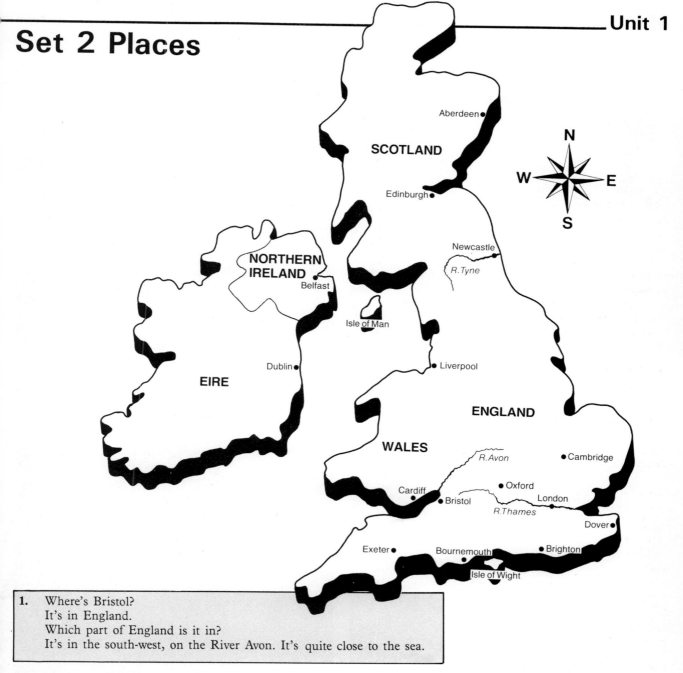

1. Where's Bristol?
   It's in England.
   Which part of England is it in?
   It's in the south-west, on the River Avon. It's quite close to the sea.

In pairs, use the map to ask and answer about:
Belfast Cardiff Newcastle Bournemouth Cambridge
Exeter Edinburgh

**Give the compass points (north, south, east, west) and say if they are
situated:**
on a river (which?)
on the coast (which?) e.g. It's on the south-west coast.
near/close to the sea
inland

2. Bristol is a large industrial and commercial city which is situated on the River Avon, in the south-west of England.

Write about the places below in the same way.

Chicago (USA)
large industrial city on
Lake Michigan in the
mid-west of the United
States

Montevideo (Uruguay)
city on the River Plate in
South America

Cortina d'Ampezzo (Italy)
large skiing village in the
Dolomite mountains

San Sebastian (Spain)
important industrial and
commercial town in the
northern part of Spain

Now write about two places in your country in the same way.

Reading

Rod Nelson is a young electrical engineer from Canada. He is working in England for a company called Western Aeronautics, which produces electrical components. It is situated in Bristol, a large city in the south-west of England.

Rod works with Jack Cooper, the production manager at Western. Jack is also a member of the trade union committee. Rod likes Jack and enjoys his job. He also likes England because it is so different from Canada. He lives in a hostel in Bristol but he wants to rent a flat of his own.

He started his job at Western in September and a few weeks later he went to dinner at the Coopers' house. There he met Barbara who is Jack and Peggy Cooper's 24-year-old daughter. She is the manageress of a shoe shop in the centre of Bristol. Rod doesn't know many people in Bristol so he enjoyed meeting her.

1. Answer:

1. What does Western Aeronautics produce?
2. Where is the factory situated?
3. What is Jack Cooper's job?
4. Does Rod like his job at Western?
5. Why does Rod like England?
6. Where does Rod live now?
7. Where does he want to live?
8. When did he start his job at Western?
9. When and where did he meet Barbara?
10. Why did Rod enjoy meeting her?

2. Western Aeronautics is a company *which* produces electrical components.

Make three similar sentences with which **using these facts:**

The company is situated in Bristol.
— employs over 500 people.
— produces components for the aircraft industry.

3. There he met Barbara *who* is Jack and Peggy's 24-year-old daughter.

Make three similar sentences with who **using these facts about Barbara:**

She is manageress of a shoe shop.
— also lives in Bristol.
— lives in a flat on her own.

4. What do you know about:

Rod Nelson? Jack Cooper? Western Aeronautics?
Barbara Cooper? The place and time Rod met Barbara?

Write sentences using, where possible:

and   but   so   because   who   which

9

Unit 1

Listening

Listen to three people from different parts of Britain talking about where they live. The first speaker comes from London. Look at the notes about her. Make similar notes about the other two people.
Write notes about yourself in the column marked YOU.

Name	Jenny	David	Mary	You
Home	student hostel		a cottage in the country	
Location	in a city (London)			
Geographical location	south-east of England			

Writing

1. Copy and fill in this personal information record.

```
              PERSONAL INFORMATION RECORD

NAME         My name is ...Marta...  STUDY DETAILS   I study English at ...
NATIONALITY  I am ...Spanish...                      ...school...
ADDRESS      My address is Marcaes                   I have studied English
             ...de Cillergelo...                     for ..7. months/terms/years.
TELEPHONE    My telephone number is..               I want to learn English for:
             ...?...                                 my job / my studies /
OCCUPATION   I am a/an ...study...                   travelling / pleasure and
                                                     interest.
                                     INTERESTS       I like ............... in my
                                                     spare time.
```

2. Write a letter to a penfriend. Write three paragraphs about yourself, your studies and your interests. Put your address at the top right-hand corner of the letter. Put the date under your address and start like this:

> International Student Hostel, Harley Street, London W1
>
> 3rd. Sept. 198-
>
> Dear Tania,
>   My name is Zlatko Tiric. I am Yugoslavian and I come from Dubrovnik. I live there in a flat with my parents. At the moment I am studying in London.

Oral exercises

1. Ask where people come from
I'm Canadian.
Oh, yes. Where in Canada do you come from?
She's English.
Oh, yes. Where in England does she come from?

1. I'm Canadian.
2. She's English.
3. He's Yugoslavian.
4. They're Italian.
5. I'm French.
6. She's Australian.

Extra work
Re-express the answers like this:
1. *Oh, so you were born in Canada.*

2. Ask where people live
Rod works in Bristol.
Oh, does he live there, too?
I study in Bristol.
Oh, do you live there, too?

1. Rod works in Bristol.
2. I study in Bristol.
3. Barbara has a shop in Bristol.
4. Paul studies in Bristol.
5. My parents both work in Bristol.

3. Say where places and things are
It is Rod's first day at Western Aeronautics.
Jack Cooper is showing him round.

Where's *your* office, by the way?
That's mine, over there.
Oh, yes. And where's *my* room?
That's yours, over there.

1. Where's *your* office, by the way?
2. Oh, yes. And where's *my* room?
3. And what about Mike's office?
4. And the secretary? Where's hers?
5. Oh, yes. Oh — where's my desk, by the way?
6. And what about yours?

4. Give correct information
Rod cannot find where places and things are.

ROD: Is that Jack's office?
GIRL: *No, Jack's office is here.*
ROD: I see. And this is the secretary's room, isn't it?
GIRL: *No, the secretary's room is here.*

1. Is that Jack's office?
2. I see. And this is the secretary's room, isn't it?
3. Oh, yes. And is that Mike's office?
4. Ah! Now, I'd like to make a phone call. Is this the secretary's telephone?
5. But this is John's office.

5. Give reasons
Why do you live in Bristol?
Because I like living in Bristol.
Why do you always get up early?
Because I like getting up early.

1. Why do you live in Bristol?
2. Why do you always get up early?
3. Why do you always cycle to work?
4. Why do you always go to bed early?
5. Why do you always study at night?
6. Why do you write letters every day?

6. Answer these questions about yourself
(Open exercise)

1. What's your name?
2. What nationality are you?
3. Where do you come from?
4. Where do you live?
5. What do you do?
6. Where do you work or study?

Open dialogue
Talk to Rod.

ROD: Hi! My name's Rod. What's yours?
YOU: ...My name is Marta.
ROD: You aren't English, are you?
YOU: ...No. I am not.
ROD: Where exactly do you come from?
YOU: ...I'm from Spanish.
ROD: What part of the country is that in?
YOU: ....
ROD: Oh, yes. I live in a hostel at the moment. What about you?
YOU: ...I live in my house.
ROD: Anyway, what do you like doing in your spare time?
YOU: ....
ROD: I see. And why do you want to learn English?
YOU: ....
ROD: Well, that's a good reason. Where do you study, by the way?
YOU: ....
ROD: Oh, there's a friend of mine over there. I'd like to talk to her. It was nice meeting you. Bye!
YOU: ....

11

Unit 2   Making friends

Dialogue

At the Coopers' house before dinner.

BARBARA: Do you like working at Western, Rod?

ROD: Yes, very much. The job's interesting and the people there are very friendly.

BARBARA: And do you mind living in a hostel?

ROD: It's all right, but I want to find a flat of my own soon. Where do you live, by the way?

BARBARA: In a flat on the other side of the city, in an old part of Bristol. What do you think of Bristol?

ROD: I like it. It's a beautiful city and the countryside around here is lovely. How do *you* like Bristol?

BARBARA: Well, it's my home town, of course. I think it's a bit depressing in winter, but it's nice in spring and autumn. Do you know many people yet?

ROD: No, not many, unfortunately.

BARBARA: Well, would you like to come and have a look round the shoe shop one day? In fact, what about coming next Saturday at lunch time? We close at one o'clock.

ROD: Thanks. That's a great idea. Why don't we have lunch together?

BARBARA: Fine. I'm not so keen on big lunches, but we could have something light.

ROD: Good. That's fixed, then.

PEGGY: Come on, you two. Dinner's ready.

Answer:
1. Does Rod like his job at Western?
2. What does he think of it?
3. What does he think of the people there?
4. Where does he live?
5. Does he like it there?
6. Where does Barbara live?
7. What does Rod think of Bristol?
8. What does he think of the countryside?
9. What does Barbara think of Bristol?
10. Does Rod know many people there?
11. What does Barbara invite Rod to do?
12. When does she suggest that he comes?
13. What does Rod suggest that they do?
14. What sort of lunch does Barbara prefer?

Set 1 Preferences

1.	Do you like cooking?	Yes, very much. It's all right. Sometimes. It depends. No, not much. No, I hate it.
	Do you mind doing housework?	No, I like it. It's all right. Sometimes. It depends. Yes, I hate it.
	Which do you prefer — cooking or washing up?	I prefer cooking (to washing up). I don't like either.

Work in pairs. Ask your partner about his/her likes and dislikes.
Write down his/her answers.

Do you like ...?	Do you mind ...?	Which do you prefer ...?
cooking going for long walks sightseeing swimming dancing reading	writing letters washing up doing housework ironing going to work getting up early staying at home on Saturday night being on your own	being with a big crowd *or* being in a small group cooking *or* washing up washing *or* ironing telephoning *or* writing letters swimming *or* going for long walks sunbathing *or* sightseeing detective stories *or* romantic novels watching video *or* going to the cinema

2. Write a few lines about your partner's likes and dislikes, like this:
Maria likes reading and sightseeing very much, but she doesn't like
cooking or doing housework. She doesn't mind getting up early or
being on her own. She prefers swimming to going for long walks.

3. Now write a few lines about yourself. Write one paragraph
   about your preferences for:
1. housework
2. household jobs
3. spare time activities

4. So you want to be:

an actor/actress?
a nurse?
an architect?
a computer operator?
a hairdresser?
a travelling
　representative?
an airline steward? *azafato*
a travel guide?
a policeman or
　policewoman?
a technician?
a security guard?

**Choose four or five jobs and write three
questions for each.**

Do you like/prefer ...?	Do you mind ...?
meeting people	working at night
driving	doing shift work
working with children	working outside
telling people what to do	wearing a uniform
talking	working long hours
travelling	working on your own
looking after people	working in an office

**In pairs, interview your partner and find out which
job would suit him/her best, like this:**
(A nurse)
Do you mind working at night?
Do you like looking after people?
Do you prefer working a normal day or doing
shift work?

14

Set 2 Opinions

> **1.** Do you like working at Western, Rod?
> Yes, very much. The job's interesting and the people there are very friendly.

Ask for an opinion	Express an opinion	Words to use	
What do you think of ...?	I think it's ... they're ... he's ... *etc.*	lovely marvellous interesting fascinating	awful boring dull depressing
How do you like ...?	I think it/he/she looks ... I like it. It's ... It's all right, but it's a bit ... I don't like it. I think it's rather ...	attractive friendly modern beautiful elegant glamorous clean	unattractive unfriendly old-fashioned ugly ordinary untidy dirty
Do you like ...?	Yes/No/I don't know. It's very ... I prefer ...	intelligent nice delicious	stupid nasty disgusting

Work in pairs. Imagine that your partner is a visitor either **to your
country** or **to Britain. Ask his/her opinions about some of these things:**
the weather   the food   the people
the way of life   the countryside   the houses
some famous buildings or well-known places

**Use the questions, phrases and words in the box above.
Make notes of your partner's answers.**

2. This is what Maria thinks about Britain.
Maria thinks the weather is nice in summer, but awful in winter,
and she doesn't like the food very much. On the other hand, she thinks
the people here are very friendly and she likes the way of life.
She prefers the houses in her own country, but she thinks that
some of the famous places like Stratford-upon-Avon are very beautiful.

Write a few sentences about your partner's opinions in the same way.

15

Unit 2

**3. Ask for and give opinions about the places
   and the people in the pictures.**

Set 3 Suggestions

1. What about coming
next Sunday?

That's a good idea!

How about meeting
for lunch?

That's a great idea!

Why don't we have
lunch together?

Well, I'm not so
keen on lunch.

Why don't we have
supper instead?
How about supper instead?
I'd rather have supper
instead.

Make a list of things to do and places to go to in your area.
Make two suggestions for:

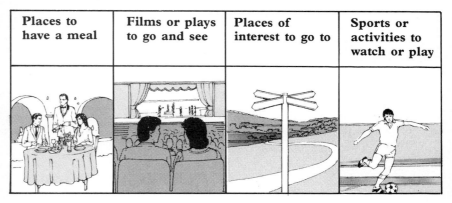

Places to have a meal	Films or plays to go and see	Places of interest to go to	Sports or activities to watch or play

Work in pairs. Suggest and agree, like this:
What about having a meal at ...?
or How about going to see ...?
        going to ...?
        watching/playing some ...?
Yes, that's a good/great idea!

2. Work in pairs. Suggest and disagree like this:
Why don't we have a meal at ...?
        go to see ...?
        go to ...?
        watch/play some ...?
Well, I'm not so keen on .... Why don't we ... instead?
                  I'd rather ... instead

3. Work in groups. Make suggestions and plans for:
a day trip to somewhere interesting
an evening out/a picnic in the country or by the sea

Plan where to go/what to do/when to meet/what food to take
or where to eat/how to get there.

Unit 2

Roleplay

It's a hot Saturday in summer. Telephone a friend and plan the day and evening out.

YOUR FRIEND

YOU

Answer the phone. Say your name.	Greet your friend and say your name.
Return greeting.	
	Suggest something to do in the afternoon.
Disagree. Say what you'd like to do instead.	
	Agree. Suggest something to do in the evening as well.
Agree. Suggest a time and place to meet in the afternoon.	
	Confirm the details. Say goodbye.
Say goodbye.	

Listening

Listen to four people saying what they think of Britain. Paul comes from Jamaica. Cindy comes from USA. Usha comes from India. Spiro comes from Greece. Make notes about what they say.

	Paul
WEATHER	Miserable, cold, damp, bleak. changeable, depressing (crudo, duro)
FOOD	rather boring, no flavour, no taste distasteful.
PEOPLE AND WAY OF LIFE	old people – snobbish (engreida) young people – alive, on fire, free

Reading

MAKING A NEW START

Every week Mike Sanders meets people who are making a new start in life. This week he meets a young Canadian.

Rod Nelson is a young, good-looking Canadian, who is on his first visit to Bristol. He comes from Ottawa and is an electrical engineer. He first trained at a college of technology and then worked for the Canadian government. Last month he arrived in Britain to start a new job with Western Aeronautics, a company which produces electrical components for the aircraft industry here in Bristol.

Why did you leave Canada?
I was bored. I worked in the same office and saw the same people and did the same thing every day. I needed a change. I wanted adventure.

Why did you choose Bristol?
I saw some photographs of Bristol in a brochure which I got from the British Tourist Association. It looked attractive. Besides, I like old cities, castles, cathedrals — things like that. Also, I like being near the sea. You see, my father was a se captain in Newfoundland. That probably why I like the sea.

What do you think of Bristol?
Actually, I like the people ver much. They're very kind an friendly. And they have a sense o humour. The way of life is ver different from Canada. It's a b slow here in Britain perhaps, but like it. And I prefer the food here – the fresh cream, the marvellou cheeses, the bread and, of course, th roast beef!

Have you any plans for the futur
So far I'm enjoying working a Western. Anyway, as there's so muc unemployment at the moment, it going to be difficult to find anoth job — in the UK at least. To tell yo the truth I'm not keen on makin plans.

Answer:
1. Where did Rod first train as an engineer?
2. Who did he work for in Canada?
3. When did he arrive in Britain?
4. Does he have any plans for the future?
5. Why not?
6. Why did he leave Canada?
7. Why did he choose Bristol?

Writing

Write a short composition about Rod Nelson. Write four paragraphs using the facts from the newspaper article.

Paragraph 1 Say who Rod Nelson is and why he is in England.
Paragraph 2 Say why he left Canada.
Paragraph 3 Say why he chose to come to Bristol.
Paragraph 4 Say what he thinks of Bristol.

Oral exercises

1. Say what you like doing (Open exercise)
What sort of things do you like doing in the summer?
I like (walking and playing tennis).
What do you like doing at home when it's raining?
I like (reading).

1. in the summer?
2. at home when it's raining?
3. reading?
4. when you go out at weekends?
5. when you go out in the evenings?
6. in your home?

Extra work
Re-express the answers, like this:
1. *I quite like (walking), but I prefer (swimming).*

2. Express likes and dislikes (Open exercise)
Do you mind getting up early?
(Yes, I do. I hate it.)
What about in the summer? Do you mind getting up early then?
(Sometimes. It depends.)
Do you mind doing housework?
(No, I don't. I like it.)

1. getting up early?
2. getting up early in the summer?
3. doing housework?
4. people smoking when you are eating?
5. people talking when you are watching TV?
6. travelling in the rush hour?
7. doing homework?
8. waiting for other people?

3. Ask if people mind doing things
A friend is thinking of becoming a policeman.

The police have to work long hours.
Well, yes. Do you mind working long hours?
They have to do shift work as well.
Well, yes. Do you mind doing shift work?

1. work long hours?
2. do shift work?
3. wear a uniform?
4. work at night?
5. tell people what to do?

4. Ask for and give opinions (Open exercise)
Ask Rod what he thinks of the weather.
YOU: *What do you think of the weather?*
ROD: It's all right, but it rains a lot. How do you like the weather in your country?
YOU: *(I like it. It's very hot in summer.)*
Ask Rod what he thinks of English food.
YOU: *What do you think of English food?*
ROD: I think it's fantastic. What do you think of the food in your country?
YOU: *(It's all right, but it's a bit dull.)*

1. the weather
2. English food
3. the way of life in England
4. the people
5. the modern buildings

5. Make suggestions
I'd like to go to the cinema this week.
Well, how about going on Monday?
And I'd like to eat out some time, too.
Well, how about eating out on Tuesday?

1. go to the cinema this week
2. eat out some time
3. go to the theatre one evening
4. drive into the country
5. visit my parents one day
6. play tennis together

6. Disagree with a suggestion and make your own suggestion (Open exercise)
What about going to see a horror film this evening?
I'm not so keen on horror films. Why don't we see (Love Story) instead?
Let's have some Chinese food first.
I'm not so keen on Chinese food. Why don't we have some (Italian) food instead?

1. see a horror film this evening
2. have some Chinese food first
3. go swimming tomorrow
4. watch TV
5. have fish for supper
6. go to the country for the weekend

Extra work
Re-express the answers, like this:
1. *I'm not so keen on horror films.*
   I'd rather see (Love Story) instead.

Unit 3 Ward fifteen

Mrs Cross is an old lady who lives in a small cottage in a village in the country outside Bristol. As she is a widow she lives alone.

Last week she had an accident. It was raining and she was walking to the village store. She slipped on the wet road, fell down, and broke her hip. By chance, a local farmer was passing on his tractor. He went back to his farm and telephoned for an ambulance.

Answer:
1. Where does Mrs Cross live?
2. Does she live alone?
3. What happened last week?
4. Where was she going?
5. How did the accident happen?
6. Was the accident serious?
7. Who helped her?
8. What did he do?

Set 1 Description: past events

1.	*What happened?*	*What was happening at the time?*
	Mrs Cross had an accident. The farmer telephoned for an ambulance.	It was raining. She was walking to the village store. A farmer was passing on his tractor.

EXPLOSION IN LONDON'S WEST END

A gas explosion at 7 o'clock last night shattered the windows of a block of flats near Hyde Park. Fortunately no one was hurt but

These are some of the people who lived in the block of flats. Look at the pictures and write what they were doing when the gas exploded.

2. Ask and answer these questions with a partner:
Where were you living two years ago?
What were you doing?
What were you doing at 6 o'clock this morning?
                9 o'clock
                yesterday evening at 10 o'clock?
What were you wearing yesterday?
Which book were you using last term?

📼 Dialogue

Mrs Cross is now in hospital. She has just had an operation on her hip. Her daughter, Joan Ingrams, comes to visit her after her operation. Joan and her family live in a house just outside Bristol.

In Ward 15.

JOAN: Hello, mum. How do you feel today?
MRS CROSS: Not too good, I'm afraid.
JOAN: Oh dear, I *am* sorry. What's the matter?
MRS CROSS: I don't know, but I've got a pain in my back now.
JOAN: Well, why don't you tell the nurse?
MRS CROSS: Yes, I will. Now how are the children?
JOAN: Oh, Mark has got a cold and a slight temperature. But he's a little better today. And Mandy's very well.
MRS CROSS: Oh, I am glad.
JOAN: Did you sleep well last night?
MRS CROSS: No, I didn't, I'm afraid. Old Mrs Grey in the next bed snored all night.
JOAN: Ssh! Mum!
MRS CROSS: Did you have a nice weekend? The weather was lovely.

JOAN: Yes, we did. We went for a walk in the country and Mandy went swimming. Oh, and we found someone for the upstairs flat. A young Canadian. He's very nice.
MRS CROSS: Oh, that's good.
JOAN: I must go back now and look after Mark. He's still got a temperature. Norman's at work, of course.
MRS CROSS: All right, dear. Give them all my love.
JOAN: I will. See you tomorrow.

Answer:

1. How does Mrs Cross feel?
2. What's the matter with her now?
3. What's the matter with Mark?
4. How is Mandy?
5. Did Mrs Cross sleep well last night?
6. What was the weather like last weekend?
7. What did the Ingrams do at the weekend?

Set 2 Health and the body

1.
A: How do you feel today?
B: Not too good, I'm afraid.
A: Oh, I *am* sorry. What's the matter?
B: I don't know, but I've got a pain in my back.

In pairs, practise the conversation choosing different parts of the body each time. Choose from:

arm   leg   shoulder   knee   foot   neck

---

2.   A: What's the matter?

B: I've got a headache.   I feel sick.
         a stomachache.   ill.
         a bad cold.   awful.
         a cough.
         a sore throat.   My head feels hot.
         a temperature.   throat feels sore.
         a pain in my back.   legs feel weak.
                      foot.
                      shoulder.
         earache.
         toothache.

A: Oh dear. I *am* sorry.
    Why don't you lie down?
                take an aspirin?
                go home?
                see a doctor?

Work in pairs. Choose something wrong with you, act it out and see if your partner can guess what the matter is. Practise like this:
A: Hello! What's the matter with you?
B: I've got a headache and I feel awful.
A: Oh, I am sorry. Why don't you take an aspirin?

---

3.   A: Is anything the matter?   A: Is anything the matter?
B: No, I'm just tired.   B: No, I'm just not hungry.
A: Yes, so am I./Are you? I'm not.   A: No, nor am I./Aren't you? I am.

In pairs, practise agreeing and disagreeing with how your partner feels in the same way. Use:
tired   not hungry   feeling sick   not feeling energetic
                             mareado.   debil.

agree → de acuerdo.
disagree → desacuerdo.

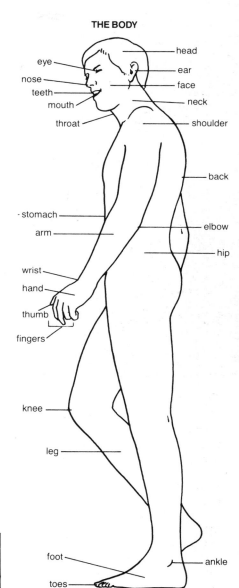

THE BODY

head
eye
ear
nose
face
teeth
neck
mouth
throat
shoulder

back

stomach
elbow
arm
hip

wrist
hand
thumb
fingers

knee

leg

foot
ankle

toes

Set 3 Health and routines

1.
A: Did you have sugar in your tea or coffee?
B: Yes, I did. I had three lumps/spoonfuls./ No, I didn't.
A: So did I./Nor did I.

Think about yesterday. Work in pairs. Complete the questionnaire. Write your own and your partner's answers. Then check your scores.

How Healthy Are You?

Check Your Diet	You	Your Partner	Score Yes	No
Yesterday...				
1. Did you have more than two pieces of toast for breakfast?			0	1
2. Did you have sugar in your tea or coffee?			0	1
3. Did you drink half a litre of milk?			1	0
4. Did you eat any fruit?			1	0
5. Did you eat any sweets or chocolates?			0	1
6. Did you eat any biscuits or cake?			0	1
7. Did you drink any alcohol?			0	1
Check Your Condition				
Yesterday...				
8. Did you go for a run?			1	0
9. Did you do any exercises?			1	0
10. Did you walk or cycle to work/school?			1	0
11. Did you smoke at all?			0	1
Check Your Daily Routine				
Yesterday...				
12. Did you get up before 8 o'clock?			1	0
13. Did you go to bed before 11 o'clock?			1	0
14. Did you watch TV for more than 2 hours?			0	1
15. Did you sleep with your windows open?			1	0
TOTAL				

How did you score?
15-12 Congratulations! You are very healthy — but don't forget to relax!
12-8 Not too bad! Keep trying!
8-0   Oh dear! Oh dear!

2.
A: I had two lumps/spoonfuls of sugar in my tea/coffee this morning.
B: Yes, so did I./Did you? I didn't.
A: I didn't drink half a litre of milk.
B: No, nor did I./Didn't you? I did.

Go through the questionnaire again with your partner. Agree or disagree each time.

24

3. What did Wilma do at 6.30?
She got up and did some exercises.

Wilma Gibson Champion Swimmer

Morning
6.30   I get up and do some exercises.
7.00   I have a glass of milk and then I go for a run in the park.
8.00   I have breakfast with my husband. I have orange juice, an egg, two bread rolls and a cup of tea with lemon.
9.15   I go to the pool and swim until lunchtime.

Afternoon
14.30 I teach swimming at the local comprehensive school.
16.00 I have a glass of milk and some fruit. Then I go home, do some housework and relax.

Evening
19.00 We have a light supper.
       Then we watch television. I go to bed about ten o'clock. But I always have a glass of milk first!

Work in pairs. What did Wilma do yesterday? Ask and answer about the different times of the day.

Write three or four sentences about Wilma's day. Start like this:
Yesterday Wilma Gibson, the swimming champion, got up at half past six and did some exercises. Then she...

Link your sentences with and or and then.
Start new sentences with Then she **or** After breakfast/lunch/school/supper she...

Writing
Now write a short composition about a day in your life.

The Perfect Pair

Jayne Torvill and Christopher Dean, Champions of ice dancing

The place: The Olympic ice rink in Helsinki
The event: The World Ice Dance Championship: (free dance section)
The people: Jayne Torvill and Christopher Dean

The crowd stands and shouts with excitement. Flowers fall like showers of rain onto the ice. The young couple hug and kiss each other as they wait for the judges' marks. And suddenly, there they are! What an incredible result — *nine* marks of 6.0! The maximum score! 'Unbelievably brilliant!', writes one journalist. 'Who can beat them now? They are not just the best, they are the best ever!'

Where did it all start? Once upon a time Jayne Torvill was a clerk in an insurance office in Nottingham. Christopher Dean was a trainee policeman. Jayne started skating when she was nine. At twelve she was the British Junior Pairs champion.

Ice skaters who take their sport seriously must give up their whole lives to their training. They start practising early, sometimes before 6 o'clock in the morning, and often do not stop until the early hours of the following morning.

When Jayne and Christopher were young, they didn't do any of the things that ordinary teenagers do. They didn't go to parties or discos. They didn't even have friends or hobbies outside the world of skating. 'You have to practise all the time,' says Jayne simply.

The families of the young skaters didn't have enough money for the expenses of ice dancing competitions. Travel, hotel bills, training costumes and skates all amount to a lot of money.

As amateur skaters, Jayne and Christopher could not earn the large sponsorship fees from big companies, but they desperately wanted to take part in major championships.

To their surprise, Jayne and Christopher received a grant of £14,000 from Nottingham City Council. With that money they were able to stop work and give their lives to skating. They began to win medal after medal.

Everyone agrees that Jayne and Christopher are two nice people. They are quiet, shy, polite and not at all spoilt by their success. 'Our aim in life is not to own a house and a car and to bring up children. It is to do something different, to achieve something special.'

The crowd of 4,000 who stood and cheered at Helsinki, and the millions of people who watched on TV, think that this is what Jayne and Christopher have already done.

1. Answer:
1. Why were Jayne and Christopher's scores at Helsinki 'incredible'?
2. How was their life different from that of ordinary teenagers?
3. In what way are Jayne and Christopher 'nice people'?
4. Why is it expensive to take part in ice skating competitions?
5. How were Jayne and Christopher able to continue their sports careers?

2. Find words or phrases in the text which mean the same as:

embrace   highest   not professional
very clever   interests   more than anything else

Use a dictionary if necessary.

Roleplay

Imagine that you are either Jayne or Christopher. In pairs, roleplay a telephone conversation with one of your parents immediately after the championships in Helsinki. Say where you are ringing from and why you are excited.

Discussion

What do you think about ice skating as a sport and ice dancing in particular?

Should people be paid if they want to take up sport as a career?

What facilities are there to take part in 'unusual' sports in your area?

▭ Listening

A reporter is talking to some athletes about their training programmes. Listen and complete the chart.

	Bo Lundquist Swedish cyclist	Anne Cole British swimmer	Bob Maley American long-distance runner
Gets up at			
Starts training at			
Finishes training at			
Spare time activities			

1. Say what's wrong with you
What's the matter with you? You don't look
very well.
I've got a temperature.
Oh, dear. Why don't you take an aspirin?
What's the matter?
I've got a headache.
Well, why don't you go to bed?

1. temperature
2. headache
3. cold
4. pain in my shoulder
5. pain in my back
6. stomachache
7. pain in my leg

Extra work
Look at the list of things that make you feel unwell in
Exercise 2 on page 23.
Choose other things wrong with you and
respond accordingly.

2. Sympathise and make suggestions
    (Open exercise)
I've got a headache.
*(Oh, I am sorry. Why don't you take an aspirin and lie
down?)*
Barbara's got an awful cold.
(Oh, dear! Why doesn't she stay in bed today?)

1. I've got a headache.
2. Barbara's got an awful cold.
3. I feel awful. My head aches. I think I've got a
   temperature.
4. Rod says he can't sleep at night.
5. Jack's got an awful pain in his back.
6. I don't know what's the matter with me. I've got an
   awful stomachache.

3. Answer questions about the recent past
    (Open exercise)
Did you go to bed early last night?
(Yes, I did. I went to bed at ten o'clock.)
Did you have a good breakfast this morning?
(No, I didn't. I only had a cup of tea.)

1. go to bed early last night?
2. have a good breakfast this morning?
3. have an English lesson yesterday?
4. do any shopping yesterday?
5. watch television yesterday?
6. do anything interesting last weekend?

4. Answer questions about Wilma Gibson's day
Did Wilma stay in bed until seven o'clock?
No, she got up and did some exercises at half past six.
What did she do after that?
*She had a glass of milk and then went for a run in the
park.*

1. Did Wilma stay in bed until seven o'clock?
2. What did she do after that?
3. Did she have breakfast alone?
4. What did she do after breakfast?
5. What did she do after lunch?
6. What did she have to eat and drink at four o'clock?
7. What did she do at home between four o'clock and
   supper time?
8. What did she and her husband do after supper?

5. Answer questions about your daily activities
    (Open exercise)
What time did you get up this morning?
I got up at (6.30).
What time did you go to bed last night?
I went to bed at (11 o'clock).

1. get up this morning?
2. go to bed last night?
3. leave home this morning?
4. get home yesterday?
5. finish work yesterday?
6. arrive here today?
7. have supper yesterday?

Extra work
Continue each exchange, like this:
1. Was it raining when you got up?
2. Was it raining when you went to bed?

6. Ask for details about the recent past
I watched TV last night.
Really? What did you watch?
I went to the theatre last week.
Really? What did you see?

1. I watched TV last night.
2. I went to the theatre last week.
3. I went to the cinema yesterday.
4. I bought a beautiful present for my mother
   yesterday.
5. I saw a friend of yours in town yesterday.
6. I had a marvellous meal last night.
7. We went to a marvellous place for our holidays.

Extra work
Re-express your comments, like this:
1. *Yes, so did I./Did you? I didn't.*

Unit 4 Two suburbs _____

All About Flowers

Car park

ABC cinem

Post Office   Lloyd's bank   Chemist

Hamburge

ELM STREET

Safeways supermarket

Scissors
hairdresser's

BIRCH STREET

The Ship

Franco's Italian restaurant

OAK STREET

Butcher's

Mr Richard clothes boutique

Library

Portland Museum

BMW garage

Taj Mahal Indian restaurant

Sutton Bros greengrocer's

Fish and

ASH STREET

Bus station

St Mary's hospital

YOU
ARE
HERE

Set 1 Facilities

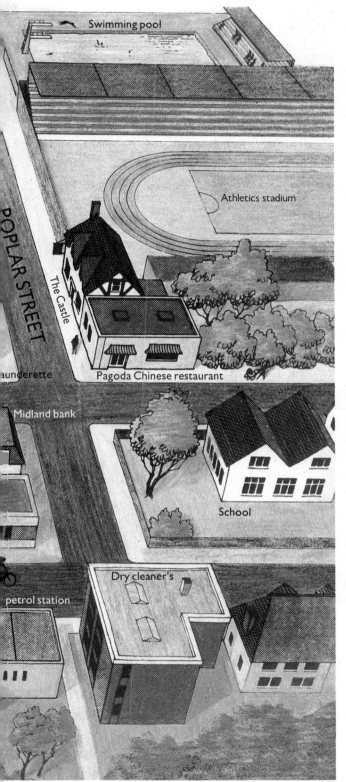

1. Is there a swimming pool
    in Portland?   Yes, there is.
    Is there a railway station? No, there isn't.
    Are there any restaurants?   Yes, there are.
                                 There are three
                                 altogether.
    Are there any tennis
    courts?   No, there aren't.

**Work in pairs. Look at this map of Portland.
Ask and answer about these facilities:**

a chemist's	pubs
a disco	nightclubs
a supermarket	restaurants
a travel agency	banks
a theatre	a hairdresser's
a park	a post office
a museum	a lake
a swimming pool	a railway station
a church	a library
a cathedral	an athletics stadium
	shopping centre

2. Is there a post office
    near here?
                              Yes, there's one on the
                              corner of Elm Street
                              and Birch Street.

    Is there a bank
    near here?
                              Yes, there are two.
                              There's one in Elm
                              Street next to the post
                              office. And one on the
                              corner of Oak Street
                              and Poplar Street.

**Work in pairs. Look at the map. Ask and say
where shops and facilities are in Portland in
the same way.**

3. **Write five sentences about shops and facilities
    in your area. Say where they are exactly.**

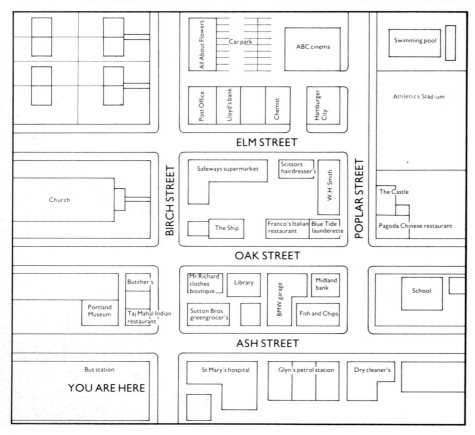

🔲 Dialogue

One Friday, Rod drove out to Portland on business. Then he realised that he needed some money for the weekend so he parked his car near the bus station.

ROD: Excuse me. Is there a bank near here?
MAN: Yes, the nearest one is in Oak Street.
ROD: I'm afraid I'm a stranger here. How do I get to Oak Street?
MAN: You walk down Birch Street as far as the first traffic lights. Then you turn right and the bank is at the end of the street on the right. In fact it's on the corner of Oak Street and Poplar Street.
ROD: I see — walk down Birch Street, turn right at the traffic lights into Oak Street and it's at the end of Oak Street on the right.
MAN: That's it. You can't miss it. It's the Midland Bank.
ROD: Fine. Thank you very much.
MAN: You're welcome.

Answer:

1. Why is Rod in Portland?
2. Why did he want a bank?
3. Where did he park his car?
4. Is he close to the bank?
5. What's the name of the bank?
6. How do you get from the bus station to the bank in Oak Street?

Set 2 Directions

1. Excuse me, but where exactly is Lloyd's Bank?
It's in Elm Street, between the post office and the chemist's.

Ask and give the exact locations of the following:
the library   the hairdresser's   a restaurant   the Midland Bank

Use any of these phrases:
next to
opposite
between the ... and the ...

2. Excuse me, but how do I get to the hamburger restaurant
in Elm Street?
You walk down Birch Street, cross over Oak Street and Elm Street is
the next street on your right. Turn right into Elm Street and
the hamburger restaurant is at the end of the street on the left.

Ask for and give directions from the bus station to the following places:
the chemist's in Elm Street
the Chinese restaurant in Oak Street
'The Castle' in Poplar Street

Use any of these phrases:
walk down
turn left/right into
cross over

... Street is the first/second/next $\left\{ \begin{array}{l} \text{street} \\ \text{turning} \end{array} \right\}$ on your left/right

walk as far as the
it's at the beginning of
      end of $\left. \begin{array}{l} \\ \\ \end{array} \right\}$ the street
      half way down

**3. Work in pairs. Ask for and give directions in Portland. Start from
the bus station each time, like this:**
Excuse me, is there a ... near here?
Yes, $\left\{ \begin{array}{l} \text{the nearest one's} \\ \text{there's one} \end{array} \right\}$ in ... Street.
How do I get to ... Street?
You ... .
I see, you ... .
That's right.
Thanks very much.
You're welcome.

**4. Draw a sketch map of your local area and mark some of the places
and streets. Work in pairs. Ask for and give directions to some of
these places. Start from a railway or bus station or another central
landmark.**

Reading

Mike Sanders, the journalist who interviewed Rod, writes about two suburbs of Bristol.

TWO SUBURBS
PORTLAND THE NEW SUTTON THE OLD

PORTLAND is a new suburb three miles east of Bristol with a population of about 25,000. It is a well-planned, modern suburb of the eighties. As well as the essential services, such as a shopping centre, a post office, banks, schools and a free bus service, there is also a library, a swimming pool, a sports complex and a cinema. There are also some good pubs and restaurants.

There is something for everybody in Portland: there are plenty of facilities and plenty of open spaces.

SUTTON — A SUBURB OF THE PAST

SUTTON, a suburb north of Bristol, with a population of about 19,000, is a typical example of a post-war, badly planned suburb. The population is large, but the essential services and the cultural, entertainments and sports facilities are poor.

NOT EVEN A GOOD RESTAURANT

Except for a few shops, a bank, a post office and a school, there are not many facilities in Sutton. There is nothing for people to do in their spare time. For example, there is no library, no cinema, no swimming pool. There are no parks or playgrounds, there isn't even a good restaurant. And there isn't even a Ladies' or Gents' public convenience in Sutton!

NOTHING TO DO

What do people do in their spare time in Sutton? Joan Little, a 22-year-old typist/clerk says, 'Nothing! There's nothing to do in Sutton. People stay at home and watch TV.'

TAKE NOTE BRISTOL COUNCIL

It is time that our local councillors — Labour, Conservative, Social Democratic, or whatever party they belong to — responded to the needs of the people. We want action in places like Sutton and we want it **NOW!** We need more well-planned places to live — places like Portland which satisfy the needs of the community.

LOCAL ELECTIONS

The local elections are next week. Your vote is important. **You** can help change Sutton into a suburb like Portland.

Answer about Portland:
1. Where is Portland situated?
2. What is the population?
3. Is it a well-planned suburb?
4. What essential services are there in Portland?
5. What facilities are there for spare time activities?

Answer about Sutton:
1. Where is Sutton situated?
2. How many people live there?
3. What do people do in their spare time in Sutton?
4. What essential services are there in Sutton?
5. Is Sutton well-planned?
6. Are there any other suburbs like this?

> **1.** As well as the essential services, there is also a library.

Link these sentences together with as well as.
1. There is a swimming pool. There is also a theatre.
2. There is a good shopping centre. There are also some small shops.
3. There are good entertainment facilities. There is also a library.

> **2.** Except for a few shops, a bank, a post office and a school, there are not many facilities in Sutton.

Link these sentences with except for.
1. There is a swimming pool. There are no other sports facilities.
2. There is a cinema. There is no other form of entertainment.
3. There is a bus service. There is no other form of transport.

3. In groups discuss the facilities and services in your areas, like this:
Is there a good bus/train/underground service?
What sports facilities are there?
What cultural and entertainment facilities are there?
There's ....   There's no/there isn't even a ....
There are ....   There are no ....
As well as ..., there's/there are ....
Except for ..., there's no/there are no ....

Writing
Read the article about Portland and Sutton on page 32 again. Make notes about the article, like this:

	PORTLAND	SUTTON	YOUR TOWN
Description:	new, modern well-planned	post-war badly-planned	
Situation:			
Population:			
Facilities— essential:			
cultural:			
entertainment:			
sports:			

Now make similar notes about your own town.

Write a short description of your town and its facilities. Use the article as a model and your notes to help you. Try to link some of your sentences with as well as **and except for.**

Unit 4

📼 Listening 1

Listen to Judith Hartley talking about the town she lives in.
Note down the facilities she talks about.

Judith talks about the following facilities:
railway station

....

📼 Listening 2

Listen to the telephone information about walks in Central London.
As you listen, trace with a pencil the directions on the map.

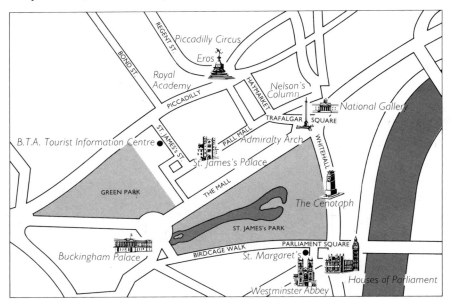

Writing

Barbara Cooper invited a friend
to come and stay for the weekend.
This is the letter she wrote.

Flat 7, 34-36 Milton Court,
Park Road, Clifton,
Bristol 8.

October 15th.

Dear Sue,

I am so glad you can come next weekend.
This is how you get to my place from the
station — it's about ten minutes walk. You
turn right outside the station and walk
down Station Road. Cross over Hatton Road
and then turn left into Weston Road.
It's the second block of flats on the
right.

Or you can take the 33 bus from the
station and get off at the corner of Weston
Road. It's only two stops from the station.
See you about 2.30 p.m.

Love, Barbara.

**Write a similar letter to a
friend. Describe how to get to
your house from the nearest
bus, railway or underground
station.**

Oral exercises

1. Ask about facilities
You need a post office.
Excuse me. Is there a post office near here?
You need a bank.
Excuse me. Is there a bank near here?

1. a post office
2. a bank
3. a launderette
4. to see a film
5. to eat out
6. to change some travellers' cheques

2. Talk about facilities
Is there a library near here?
Yes. There's a very good library over there.
Is there a restaurant near here?
Yes. There's a very good restaurant over there.

1. a library
2. a restaurant
3. a pub
4. a hairdresser's
5. a chemist's
6. a Chinese restaurant

3. Answer questions about facilities
Look at the map of Portland.
You are at the bus station in Birch Street.

Is there a bank near here?
*Well, there isn't a bank in this street, but there's one
in Oak Street (And there's one in Elm Street.)*
Thanks.
Is there a pub near here?
*Well, there isn't a pub in this street, but there's one
in Poplar Street. (And there's one in Oak Street.)*
Thanks.

1. a bank
2. a pub
3. a launderette
4. a hairdresser's
5. a hamburger restaurant
6. a cinema
7. a Chinese restaurant

4. Talk about facilities
You are in Sutton.

I'm looking for a hairdresser's.
Well, there aren't any hairdressers' here.
I'm looking for a cinema.
Well, there aren't any cinemas here.

1. a hairdresser's
2. a cinema
3. a library
4. a park
5. a swimming pool
6. a playground

Extra work
Re-express your answers, like this:
1. *Well, there are no hairdresser's here.*

5. Ask for directions
You want to know the way to the supermarket.
Excuse me. How do I get to the supermarket?
You want to know the way to the swimming pool.
Excuse me. How do I get to the swimming pool?

1. the supermarket
2. the swimming pool
3. the bus station
4. the ABC cinema
5. the post office

6. Repeat directions
You turn right and then left.
I see. I turn right and then left.
You walk down this road and then you turn right.
I see. I walk down this road and then I turn right.

1. You turn right and then left.
2. You walk down this road and then you turn right.
3. You cross over this road and take the first on your
   left.
4. You take the second right and then right again.
5. You turn left, then right and then left again.
6. You take the third on the left and then cross over
   the square.

Unit 5 A place of my own

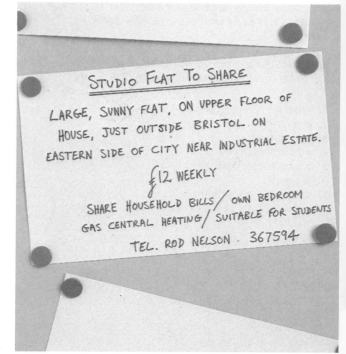

When Rod first started his job in Western, he stayed in the factory hostel. The hostel only served breakfast, so Rod had lunch in the canteen at work. When he finished work, he usually went to a cheap self-service restaurant for his evening meal.

He didn't enjoy living in the hostel very much, so he decided to find a flat to rent. He soon found one just outside Bristol. It was quite a big flat on the top floor of a house owned by Joan and Norman Ingrams. Because the rent was more than he could afford, and there were two bedrooms, Rod decided to find someone to share the flat with him. One morning he put an advertisement in the local newsagent's window.

The same day, a young student called Paul Blake went to the newsagent to buy a paper. When he saw the advertisement, he telephoned Rod immediately and asked permission to come and see the flat.

1. Answer:
1. Where did Rod stay when he first started at Western?
2. What meals did he have there?
3. Where did he have his other meals?
4. Why did he decide to find a flat?
5. Where was the flat situated?

2. Paul saw the advertisement. Then he telephoned Rod immediately.

=

When Paul saw the advertisement, he telephoned Rod.

Link these sentences using when.
1. He got home. Then he telephoned Rod.
2. He found his address book. Then he wrote Rod's name in it.
3. He telephoned Rod. Then he asked permission to come and see the flat.

3. Link your answers with when, so, because, and, but **or** then.
1. Why did Rod decide to rent a flat of his own?
2. What did he do?
3. What happened?

🔲 Dialogue

ROD: 367 594. Rod Nelson speaking.

PAUL: Oh, hello. My name's Paul Blake. I'm ringing about the flat.

ROD: Oh, yes. You saw my ad in the newsagent's, did you?

PAUL: That's right. Could you tell me something about the flat?

ROD: Well, there's quite a big sitting room — and a kitchen.

PAUL: What about bedrooms?

ROD: Oh, there are two bedrooms — one big and one a bit smaller, but it's quite nice.

PAUL: I see. So I'd have my own bedroom?

ROD: Yes.

PAUL: Er...what about the rent? How much is it exactly?

ROD: Well, I pay thirty pounds a week.

PAUL: Thirty pounds!

ROD: Yes, but I thought I would pay eighteen pounds and ask the other person to pay twelve. Because, you know, er, because I've got the big bedroom. That seems only fair. Look, why don't you come round and see the flat? Then you can make up your own mind. It's better than trying to talk about it over the phone.

PAUL: Yes, er . . . may I come round and see it straightaway — like, now, this morning?

ROD: Well, actually, it's a bit difficult for me this morning. I've got to go out.

PAUL: Well, may I come and see it this afternoon? At about three?

ROD: Yes, do. Three would be fine for me.

PAUL: What's the address?

ROD: 57 Bath Road.

PAUL: Oh, I know Bath Road. It's quite near where I live now.

Answer:
1. Is Paul a friend of Rod's?
2. Does Rod's flat have only one bedroom?
3. How much rent does Rod pay?

🔲 Listening

Now listen to an extended version of the telephone conversation between Rod and Paul.

Answer True or False
1. Not all the rooms are on the same floor.
2. Paul is a student at a polytechnic.
3. He studies electrical engineering and maths.
4. He decided to go and see the flat on Saturday afternoon.
5. The address is 57 London Road.
6. Paul will need two keys.
7. The Ingrams do not live in the house.

Set 1 Permission

1. *Ask permission formally*   *Give permission formally*

May I
Do you mind if I } come and see the flat?
Is it all right if I

Yes, of course.
Yes, certainly.

Ask permission informally   *Give permission informally*

Can I come and see the flat?

Yes, sure.
Yes, do.

Work in pairs. Ask for and give permission to do these things, first formally, then informally:

sit on the balcony   close the blinds
open the door   turn off the light
borrow your book   turn on the television
use your telephone

2. *Ask permission formally*   *Refuse permission formally*

Do you mind if I
May I } use your phone?
Is it all right if I

Well, actually, I'm expecting a phone call myself.

Ask permission informally   *Refuse permission informally*

Can I use your phone?

Sorry, but I'm expecting a phone call myself.

Work in pairs. Use the suggestions below to ask for and refuse permission, first formally, then informally. Refuse with a different reason each time.

— smoke	This is a non-smoking compartment. There's a no smoking sign. I feel sick when people smoke.
— come and see you this evening	Guests are coming for supper. I want to go to bed early.
— telephone you at work	I haven't got a phone in my office. It's against the rules.
— open the window	It's very noisy when it's open. I've got an awful cold and it's freezing outside.
— borrow your car	There's no petrol in it. It's being serviced.
— play your new Michael Jackson record	I lent it to my sister. The amplifier is broken.

3. Ruth, a good friend of Barbara's, comes to see her one day after work. Ruth usually does what she wants, but she always asks permission first. Complete the conversation using the following phrases:

Can I ...?
Yes, sure!
Yes, do!
Sorry, but ....

BARBARA: Ruth! How nice to see you! Come in!
RUTH: Thanks. Phew! I'm exhausted. It's been a hard day ....?
BARBARA: .... That's the comfortable chair over there.
RUTH: Great! Thanks. Oh, what's the time, by the way?
BARBARA: Quarter past six.
RUTH: Oh, dear. Is it? I must give Terry a call ....?
BARBARA: .... It's in the hall.
RUTH: Thanks.
(She goes to ring Terry. A few minutes later she comes back.)
Terry sends his regards.
BARBARA: Oh, thanks.
RUTH: What's that book, Barbara?
BARBARA: Oh, sorry. It's the new John le Carré novel. I'm still reading the last chapter. It's very exciting.
RUTH: ....?
BARBARA: .... I promised to lend it to Bob.
RUTH: Oh, that's all right. Barbara, I would love a cup of coffee ....?
BARBARA: .... You know where the kitchen is. Why don't you make me one, too?
RUTH: OK. And then you must tell me all about Rod. Didn't you say he's rather good-looking?

Roleplay

Act these situations with a partner. What do you say to:

— a stranger when you want to look at his/her newspaper on the train?
— a friend who has the radio on at full volume when you've got a headache?
— strangers when you need to make a phone call in their house?
— a friend when you want to talk to him/her alone about a personal problem?

Set 2 Description: house and furniture

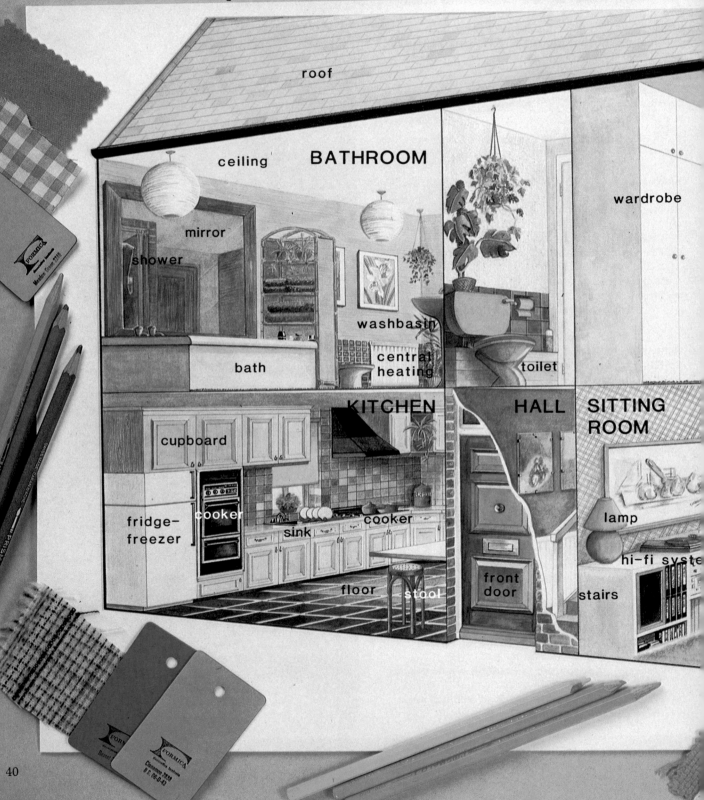

roof

ceiling

BATHROOM

mirror

shower

wardrobe

washbasin

bath

central heating

toilet

KITCHEN

HALL

SITTING ROOM

cupboard

lamp

cooker

hi-fi syste

fridge-freezer

cooker

sink

stairs

front door

floor

stool

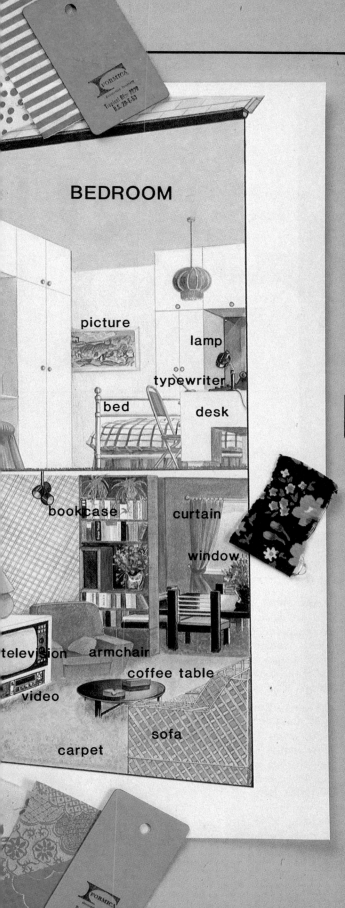

BEDROOM

picture

lamp

typewriter

bed

desk

bookcase

curtain

window

television

armchair

coffee table

video

sofa

carpet

1. **What furniture and fittings are there in the bedroom/kitchen/sitting room of this house? Answer like this:**

In the bedroom, there's a ...

2. **Write a short description of the house, like this:**

This is quite a big house. There is an upstairs and a downstairs.

Downstairs there is a ... *(name rooms)* and upstairs there's a ... and a ... *(name rooms)*. In the bedroom upstairs there's a ... *(name furniture)*. Downstairs in the sitting room there's a ... *(name furniture)*. In the kitchen there's a ... *(name furniture, etc)*.

3. Either **write down the names of the rooms in your house or flat and what furniture and fittings there are in each of them,** or draw a **plan of your house or flat and label all the rooms and furniture.**

---

4.   The table is made of wood/glass.
     The chair is made of plastic/leather/a soft material.

Think of your bedroom or sitting room at home. Work in pairs. Ask and answer questions like:
What about the carpet?
What furniture is there in the room?
(Describe it — size, texture, colour, shape, material.)
What colour are the walls?
What are the curtains like? What colour are they?

5. **Write a paragraph describing one of the rooms in this house and the furniture in it. Say if you like the room. Give reasons.**

SIZE	large	small	high	low		
TEXTURE	hard	soft	heavy	light		
COLOUR	dark light	red	blue	green	yellow	purple
	black white	grey	brown	orange	pink	beige
PATTERN	plain	flowery	striped	checked		
SHAPE	round	oval	square	rectangular		
MATERIAL	wood	metal	plastic			
	leather	glass	material			

41

Reading

Those difficult requests

I was on a train the other day, travelling from London to Bristol. I was sitting in an empty compartment, and I wanted to read the last chapter of my murder mystery. Suddenly the door opened and a woman with a baby and two noisy children came in. The children immediately climbed onto the seats. 'May we join you?' said the woman. At first I wanted to say, 'Well, actually, I'm reading a very exciting book and I'd like to finish it. Could you possibly find another compartment?'

But of course, I smiled a charming smile and said, 'Yes, certainly.' I still have not finished that last chapter and I still don't know who the murderer is. You see, I am unfortunately one of those people who find it difficult to say 'No' to those magic words, 'May I ...'. or 'Do you mind if I ...'.

In this polite world of ours people usually ask permission to do quite harmless things, like use the telephone, turn the light on, take their coats off, open the window and things like that. Some people even ask permission to use the lavatory, or if they may wash their hands. (On the other hand, I believe that very few smokers will bother to ask permission to smoke!)

But what about those *difficult* requests like, 'Can I use your phone for a moment. I promised to ring my grandparents in Edinburgh tonight?' (when *you* live in Bristol). Or, 'Do you mind if I come round and watch your TV? Mine's broken.' (when you are busy with your income tax forms). Or, when you invite an elderly aunt and uncle to spend Easter or Christmas with you and they say, 'Is it all right if we bring our cat — he gets so lonely with the neighbours?' (when you have got a rather bad-tempered dog in your house). The trouble is that when I hear those magic words, I just don't have the courage to refuse. Well, what do *you* say to those difficult requests?

Answer:

1. Find three examples in the text of:

   a) harmless requests
   b) difficult requests

2. What happened on the train?
   The author was in an empty ...

3. Do people in your country ask permission to smoke, use the phone, or help themselves to something to drink in a friend's house? What other things do people ask permission to do?

Listening

Listen to these two people describing their bedrooms. Make notes as you listen.

	Furniture, etc	Description (size/colour, etc)
Kevin		
Sally		

Discussion

You decide to turn your classroom into a student recreation room. Discuss what furniture/curtains/carpet/colour scheme you would like.
Draw a plan of the room as you would like to see it. Label the furniture and show your plan to the other groups. Use expressions like:

I'd like to have a coffee machine.
Why don't we get a ...?
What about } buying { a ...?
How about } buying { some ...?
Yes, that's a good idea.
No, I'm not so keen on ...
I'd rather have ...

Writing

Write a few paragraphs describing your ideal recreation room.

Oral exercises

1. Ask for permission informally and formally

You are in a friend's house. You want to use the phone.
Can I use the phone?
Yes, do.
You are at your boss's house. You want to use the bathroom.
May I use the bathroom?
Yes, of course.

1. You are at a friend's house. You want to use the phone.
2. You are at your boss's house. You want to use the bathroom.
3. You are at your parents' house. You want to watch television.
4. You are on a train. You want to borrow a newspaper from another passenger.
5. You are at a friend's house. You want to make a cup of tea.
6. You are in a crowded café. There is only one seat next to an old lady. You want to sit down.
7. You are at a friend's house. You want to play some records.

Extra work

Re-express the formal requests for permission using *'Do you mind if I ...?'* or *'Is it all right if I ...?'*

2. Refuse permission formally and informally
   (Open exercise)
May I come and see you this evening?
Well, actually, (I've got guests for supper).
Can I smoke here?
Sorry, but (I feel sick when people smoke).
1. May I come and see you this evening?
2. Can I smoke here?
3. Can I telephone you at work?
4. May I open the window?
5. Can I borrow your car?
6. May I play your new Abba record?

3. Describe things
What shape is an apple?
Round.
What colours are the British flag?
Red, white and blue.

1. What shape is an apple?
2. What colours are the British flag?
3. What's a record made of?
4. What shape is a football field?
5. What's a football made of?
6. What's a window made of?
7. What shape is a chessboard?
8. What colours are your country's flag?

4. Comment on colours
A friend is describing her new house to you.

What colour's the house?
Green and white.
Mm. A green and white house. That sounds nice.
What colour's the kitchen?
Yellow.
Mm. A yellow kitchen. That sounds nice.

1. What colour's the house? (Green and white)
2. What colour's the kitchen? (Yellow)
3. What colour are the kitchen curtains? (Green and white checked)
4. What about the sitting room? What colour are the walls? (Dark blue)
5. And the carpet? (Plain white)
6. What about the curtains? (Pink and white striped)

5. Ask about furniture
You are going to rent a house for a month. You ring the house agent to see what there is in the house. Look at the plan on page 40.

Ask about a sofa.
Is there a sofa in the sitting room?
Oh, yes.
Ask about a fridge.
Is there a fridge in the kitchen?
Of course.

Ask about:

1. a sofa
2. a fridge
3. a wardrobe
4. a cooker
5. a washbasin
6. a record player

Unit 6 Consolidation

❶ 🔊 Dialogue

Joan Ingrams calls in to see her neighbour, Pat, one Saturday morning.

JOAN: Hello, Pat. Are you busy?

PAT: Oh, hello, Joan. Come in. No, I'm not busy.

JOAN: How do you feel now? How's your cold?

PAT: Oh, much better, thanks.

JOAN: Oh, good. I *am* glad. Look, would you like to come into town with me this morning and buy some curtain material?

PAT: Yes, I'd love to. What about going to Barker's? They usually have good materials.

JOAN: Mm. I'm not so keen on Barker's. It's so expensive there. But there's a good shop which sells materials in Patton Street. It's called Bailey's.

PAT: Bailey's. I don't know it. How do you get to it?

JOAN: Well, you walk down Broad Street and turn right at the second traffic lights, and then you're in Patton Street. Bailey's is about half way down on the left.

Later that morning in Bailey's.

GIRL: Can I help you? Or are you just looking?

JOAN: Well, yes, actually. I'm looking for some plain curtain material. Dark blue, I think.

GIRL: Well, the plain materials are over there. Why don't you have a look? I'll be back in a minute.

JOAN: Thank you. What do you think of this, Pat?

PAT: Mm. It's all right. But it isn't dark blue.

JOAN: No, and it's rather expensive.

GIRL: Have you found anything you like?

JOAN: Er...I'm not sure. May I take a sample of this material?

GIRL: Yes, of course. Here you are.

JOAN: Thank you very much.

GIRL: You're welcome.

JOAN: *(to Pat)* Let's go to Barker's after all!

1. Answer:

1. What day of the week is it?
2. What has been the matter with Pat?
3. What does Joan want to do?
4. Why does she think Bailey's is better than Barker's?
5. Which street is Bailey's in?
6. How do you get there from Broad Street?
7. What colour material is she looking for?
8. What is wrong with the material she looks at?
9. Does she buy it?
10. Where do they go after that?

2. Practise the dialogue in threes.

3. In the dialogue, find examples of how to:

greet someone informally
ask about someone's health
answer about one's health
invite someone to do something
accept an invitation
make a suggestion
disagree
talk about a facility/service
ask for directions
give directions
describe what one is looking for
ask for an opinion
express an opinion
ask for permission to do something
give permission
thank someone
respond to thanks

4. Roleplay

1. You call on a friend and invite him/her to come with you to buy a pair of trousers/jeans/or a dress.
2. Discuss where to go and how to get there.
3. In the shop, ask your friend's opinion about the clothes you look at.
4. Ask the shop assistant's permission to try the clothes on.
5. If you like the clothes, ask how you can pay for them, e.g. by cheque, credit card, or with cash.
6. If you do not like the clothes, thank the assistant politely and leave.

2 Reading

SEASIDE IS TOPS

When the sky is blue and the sun is shining, British people like to get out into the open air. In particular, they like to go to the seaside for their ideal day out. According to a new nationwide survey, two thirds of all the children and nearly half of all the adults in the survey put going to the seaside at the top of a list of things they would like to do on a sunny day in summer.

Walks and drives in the country are favourite alternatives for adults. Children, however, prefer going to sports events, seeing friends or going on a trip to London.

A third of the children like the idea of a country walk or going to a safari park or zoo, but only one in ten put it as their favourite activity. Not surprisingly, visiting stately homes* is more popular with adults than children. Almost one in five adults enjoys visiting stately homes.

What makes a day out enjoyable for many children and adults too, is an ice cream or lolly. This is especially true of children for over half of them prefer ice cream to soft drinks, fish and chips, hamburgers, sweets and chocolates.

For most youngsters the attraction of ice cream is that it is refreshing and tastes good. More than three quarters say that these are the things they like most about it.

Not surprisingly, the majority of adults put visiting the pub for a drink top of their day out enjoyment, although they also like ice cream and for the same reasons as children.

Nearly three out of ten family outings in the summer involve journeys of more than 50 miles. Most families on a day out set off before 11 a.m. but some get started before 9 a.m. The majority return home after 6 p.m.

SUMMER OUTING CHOICES

The thing they would 'most like to do' on a sunny day

Children's ranking		Adults' ranking
1	THE SEASIDE	1
2	SPORTS EVENT	4
3=	VISITING FRIENDS	6=
3=	LONDON TRIP	8=
5	COUNTRY WALK	2
6	SAFARI PARK OR ZOO	10=
7=	DRIVE IN COUNTRY	3
7=	PICNIC	6=
9=	STAY AT HOME	5
9=	VISIT RELATIVES	8=
11	MUSEUM/ART GALLERY	12
0	STATELY HOME	10=

1. **Answer True or False**
   (Look at the photograph, the text and the chart.)

   1. The photograph was taken in the winter.
   2. The girl is eating an ice lolly.
   3. The British prefer going out in the country for an ideal day out.
   4. Children have the same preferences as adults when choosing leisure activities.
   5. Adults like visiting stately homes more than children do.
   6. Children prefer sweets and chocolates to ice cream.
   7. Adults like eating ice cream for the same reasons as children.
   8. Most people in Britain set out very early in the morning (before 9 a.m.) when they go on a day's outing.
   9. Adults prefer driving in the country to going to sports events.
   10. Children like visiting stately homes.

2. **Make a list of all the expressions to do with amounts and number, e.g.** most, all, two thirds, **etc. and arrange them in order of size.**

3. **Project**
   Conduct a survey of the preferences of your group for a day's outing. Look at the list of summer outings in the chart and put them in order according to your preferences. Compare your lists and discuss any differences.

4. **Discussion**
   Is the list of summer outings different from the one that people in your country might make? How is it different?

45

Palaces, mansions and large houses which are open to the public

Unit 6

3 **Complete the conversational exchanges.**

1. A: ....?
   No, I'm not.
   A: ....?
   B: From Belgium.

2. A: ....?
   B: No, not much. My husband does most of the cooking.

3. A: ....?
   B: It's all right. But London is like most big cities — noisy, dirty and depressing if you don't know anyone.

4. A: Shall we go to the Flamingo Club this evening?
   B: ....
   A: Well, *what* shall we do then? I'm bored.
   B: ....?
   A: But there's nothing good on at the cinema this week.

5. A: ....?
   B: I've got a headache, that's all.
   A: ....?

6. A: ....?
   B: Oh, much better, thank you.
   A: ....

7. A: ....?
   B: No, not very well, I'm afraid. You see, I never sleep well in a strange bed.

8. A: ....?
   B: Yes, we did, thanks. A lovely weekend.
   A: ....?
   B: We went to see some friends in Exeter.

9. A: ....?
   B: Yes, there's one in Broad Street. It sells all sorts of records — classical, pop, rock, jazz — everything.

10. A: ....?
    B: You take the 67 bus to the corner of Broad Street and then walk. The library is halfway down the street on the left-hand side.

11. A: ....?
    B: Yes, of course. I think the News starts in five minutes.

12. A: May I use your phone for a minute?
    B: .... I'm expecting a call from France any minute now.

4 📼 **Listening**

Listen to this young man talking about his job. He will give you five clues. If you can guess his job after the first clue, write it down. If you are right, you score five points. If you can't guess, listen to the next clue. If you guess right, you score four points and so on.

Clue 1 (5 points): ....
2 (4 points): ....
3 (3 points): ....
4 (2 points): ....
5 (1 point): ....

5 📼 **Listening**

Listen to a telephone conversation at Western Aeronautics. Lynne Thomas, a secretary, answers the phone and takes a message. Listen and write down the message.

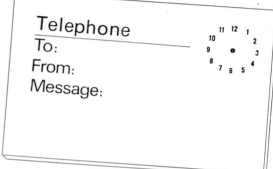

Telephone
To:
From:
Message:

6 **Roleplay**

Work in pairs. Your partner is a visitor to your home town. You are a reporter for a local newspaper. You are going to write an article about foreigners' opinions about your home town. Interview your partner. Find out:

1. his/her name and nationality
2. why he/she is visiting your home town
3. his/her opinions about it
4. what he/she likes doing in his/her spare time.

Then:

1. Suggest a meeting with him/her for lunch later in the week.
2. Name a place to meet.
3. Give directions to get there.

7 **Writing**

Write about the last holiday you had. Write:

1. where you went
2. what part of the country it was
3. what the countryside/surroundings were like
4. where you stayed
5. what you did while you were there
6. what your opinion of the holiday was.

8 Group work

Some American visitors are visiting your country for the first time next summer. They are Robert Selinker and his wife, Louise, with their children, Barbi aged 15 and Matt aged 19. Both Robert and Louise like sightseeing and eating food from other countries. Louise is interested in photography, too. Barbi likes sport and Matt likes dancing. Plan an interesting holiday for the Selinker family.

Make suggestions like this:

Why don't we { take them to ...?
{ show them ...?
Let's take Matt/Barbi to ...?
What about visiting ...?
How about going to ...?

9 Games

Remember! Remember!

You have 5 minutes. Write down as many
    COLOURS,
    PIECES OF FURNITURE,
    SHAPES
and MATERIALS as you can remember!

Twenty Questions

One person thinks of a piece of furniture or object. The others must try to guess what it is in less than 20 questions. They can only ask questions with a 'Yes' or 'No' answer. Like this:

Is it red?
Is it made of plastic?
etc.

Unit 7 Guests for supper___

🔊 Dialogue

Rod and Paul have invited Barbara and Sue, Paul's girlfriend, to supper. They are in the kitchen getting supper ready.

PAUL: What have we got in the fridge, Rod?

ROD: Nothing much. We've got some ham, eggs, cheese...

PAUL: Have we got any potatoes?

ROD: I think so. Yes, we have. And we've got some onions, too.

PAUL: Well, why don't we have some ham and a Danish potato salad? I copied down the recipe from the radio yesterday.

A few minutes later.

ROD: Let's see now. Cut the potatoes into small cubes...

PAUL: Yes, but don't cut them yet. Wait until they're cool. Where's the big red plastic bowl?

ROD: On the bottom shelf in the cupboard under the sink.

PAUL: What's Barbara like, by the way?

ROD: Barbara? Well, she's in her mid-twenties. She's very lively. She's got a good sense of humour. I think you'll like her. What about Sue?

PAUL: Oh, Sue's very easy-going and friendly.

ROD: Could you get me the mayonnaise from the cupboard?

PAUL: Yes, sure. Which cupboard is it in?

ROD: It's in the small one beside the cooker.

PAUL: There's no mayonnaise here.

ROD: Oh, isn't there? Oh, no! The recipe says parsley and lemon. I know we haven't got ...

Doorbell rings.

They're here!

BARBARA: Hello! Here we are! You're Paul, are you? What's the matter? You both look miserable!

PAUL: We're making a potato salad and...

ROD: ...we haven't got any mayonnaise, or parsley or lemon!

SUE: Well, that's all right. I'm on a diet.

BARBARA: And I *hate* potato salad. So that's fine. Here, I've got some wine. Let's have a glass now!

Answer:

1. What have Rod and Paul got in the fridge?
2. What does Paul suggest they have for supper?
3. Where is the big red plastic bowl?
4. How does Rod describe Barbara?
5. How does Paul describe Sue?
6. Where does Rod say the mayonnaise is?
7. Have they got any?
8. What else haven't they got?
9. Why do Paul and Rod both look miserable?

Set 1 Household provisions and utensils

1. Have we got any milk? Yes, we've got lots of milk.
   Have we got any meat? No, we haven't.

Work in pairs. Look at the kitchen list. Ask and answer like this:
Have we got any ...?
Yes, we've got lots of ....
No, we haven't.

2. Have we got anything to
   eat?   We've got some bread.
   What else have we got?   We've got some cheese.
   What else?

Look at the list again. Ask and answer in the same way.

3. What else have we got? What about tinned tomatoes?
   No, we haven't got any tinned tomatoes.
   What about meat?
   No, we haven't got any meat.

Look at the things on the list marked with an X. Ask and answer in the same way.

4. **Look at the list and say what you have or haven't got at home. Choose only a few things from the list, like this:**
I've got some milk, butter and cheese, but I haven't got any fish or meat.

5. Where are the knives
   and forks?   In the drawer beside the cooker.
   Which drawer?   The top one.
   Where are the cups?   In the cupboard on the top shelf on the left.

Work in pairs. Ask and say exactly where everything is.

cups and saucers	knives, forks and spoons
plates	kitchen knives
bowls	wooden spoons
saucepans	

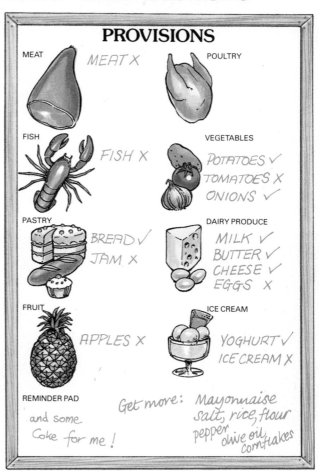

PROVISIONS

MEAT — *MEAT X*
POULTRY
FISH — *FISH X*
VEGETABLES — *POTATOES ✓ TOMATOES X ONIONS ✓*
PASTRY — *BREAD ✓ JAM X*
DAIRY PRODUCE — *MILK ✓ BUTTER ✓ CHEESE ✓ EGGS X*
FRUIT — *APPLES X*
ICE CREAM — *YOGHURT ✓ ICE CREAM X*
REMINDER PAD — *and some Coke for me!*
Get more: Mayonnaise salt, rice, flour pepper olive oil cornflakes

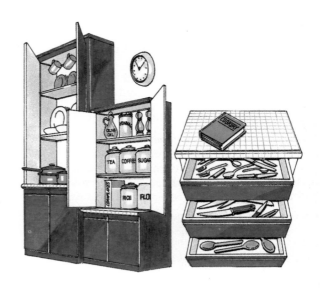

Set 2 Requests

> **1.** Could you get me the mayonnaise from the
> cupboard, please?
> Yes, sure.

**Ask your partner to get you the following things
from the supermarket:** milk, eggs, rice, cornflakes,
salt, apples.

Ask and answer like this:

I'm going to the supermarket. Do you want anything?
Oh, yes. Could you get me some butter, please?
Yes, sure. Do you want anything else?
Yes. Could you get me some ... as well?

2. Look at these shops.

**Make a list of the things you want from each
shop, like this:**

Greengrocer's: lettuce, beans, onions, oranges
Sweetshop:
Newsagent's:
Chemist's:

Then work in pairs, like this:

A: I'm going to the greengrocer's. Do you want
anything?
B: Oh, yes. Could you get me some beans, some
onions and a lettuce, please? And could you get me
some oranges as well?

Listening 1

Listen to these four short conversations. In each
one, someone asks another person to do something.
The first conversation is complete; the other three
have gaps. Write down the sentence that you think
will fill the gap in each conversation, like this:

Conversation 1: Could you give me a lift to the
station?

Conversation 2:
Conversation 3:
Conversation 4:

Listening 2

Listen to the instructions for making Danish Potato Salad on the tape and number the pictures in the correct order. Write 1 by the first step, 2 by the second step and so on. When the instructions are in the right order, write them out in full, like this:

Instructions for making a Danish Potato Salad
First peel and cook ...
Next ...
Then ...

Danish Potato Salad

Sprinkle with parsley.

Fold in tablespoon of chopped parsley.

Mix ½ tablespoon of lemon juice with the seasoned mayonnaise.

Peel and cook 1kg. of potatoes in salted boiling water. Leave to cool.

Finely chop onions.

Chill in fridge.

Cut potatoes into small cubes.

Mix potatoes and onions into mayonnaise.

You need 1kg. potatoes, 2 large onions, mayonnaise, lemon juice, parsley, salt and pepper.

Danish Potato Salad

INGREDIENTS (for 6 people):

1 kg potatoes
2 large onions
2½ dl mayonnaise

½ tbsp fresh lemon juice
chopped parsley
salt and pepper

51

Set 3 Instructions and advice

A HOLIDAY IN THE SUN? LOVELY! BUT BE CAREFUL!

As the holiday season approaches it seems sensible to remind holiday makers of the dangers of taking too many risks with the sun and the sea.

Consuela Fernandez, a Spanish hotel owner from Sitges on the Costa Brava, a popular spot with British tourists, says, 'Holiday visitors! Sometimes they are stupid! They go straight to the beach on their first day and lie in the sun too long. Then they are miserable because they have to stay inside for a few days. Why don't people listen to advice? It is extremely important to be careful with the sun during the first few days of your holiday. It is better to sunbathe for just half an hour during the first few days and then increase the amount of time daily.

And it's stupid to go to the beach in the middle of the day, when the sun is very hot. The morning is better — or late afternoon.

People take risks with the sea, too. Many people swim immediately after a heavy lunch. This can be dangerous because you can get cramp in your legs and arms and drown.

It is also unwise to take passports, travel documents and tickets with you when you go shopping or sightseeing. It is much better to put all your valuables in the hotel safe. This is what I always tell my guests. It is better to be safe than sorry! But they seldom take any notice.

Of course it's common sense. But tourists seem to leave their common sense at home when they go on holiday!'

Holiday advice
some practical hints for people o holiday

about Travellers' Cheques
1. **Carry** your passport, your money and Travellers' Cheques in a safe place — not in a beach bag, or all in one pocket or wallet.
2. **Check** rates of exchange when you cash your cheque — shops or hotels may legitimately lower the rate a little; make sure it is only a little!
3. **Fill in** the detachable slip in your Travellers' Cheque book and keep this record of your cheque numbers in another place.
4. **Don't** countersign unless yo are in the presence of the person who is changing the cheque.
5. **Keep** some Travellers' Cheques or notes in reserve for emergencies, otherwise you may be in the awful position of finding yourself abroad and flat broke.
6. **Expect** to present some proo of your identity when cashing Travellers' Cheques. Don't forget to take your passport with you.

about money
7. **Don't** carry a large amount of cash with you. If someon steals it or you lose it, you

are not likely to get it back. Carry enough cash for your day-to-day expenses. If you are staying in a hotel, give any large amounts of cash to the manager to put in the hotel safe and get a receipt.

bout personal possessions

8. **Don't** wear expensive jewellery or watches when you go out.

9. **Don't** leave your handbag unattended even for short periods. Always take it with you or ask a friend to look after it.

0. **Don't** leave hand luggage, including your briefcase, unattended on railway platforms, waiting rooms, luggage racks or anywhere else. You should carry valuables such as a camera, radio, or portable typewriter and you should keep a note of the serial numbers. You should take special care of your passport, plane tickets and other personal documents.

bout self-service shops

1. **Always** use the baskets or trolleys in self-service shops or supermarkets. Always pay for goods *before* leaving the shop. Failure to do so is very likely to lead to arrest, police prosecution, and a fine or even prison for shoplifting.

1. Answer True or False
1. Sitges is a seaside resort.
2. Consuela thinks that most tourists are intelligent and wise.
3. She says that people often spoil their holidays because they lie in the sun too long.
4. Consuela thinks that midday is the best time to go to the beach.
5. It is dangerous to go swimming after a big meal.
6. The beach is a good spot for thieves to work.

2. Use the information in the magazine article to make a list of instructions for people on holiday. Start like this:
1. Don't lie in the sun too long on your first day. Sunbathe for just half an hour during the first few days. Increase the amount of time daily.
2. Don't go to .....

---

3. You shouldn't lie too long in the sun.
You should sunbathe for just half an hour the first day.

In pairs, use your list of instructions to give each other personal advice using should **or** shouldn't.

4. Read the list of holiday advice and find words which mean the same as the following:

legally	extra	money
bring down	situation	expensive items
certain	without any money	result in

Writing

Write two or three paragraphs giving advice to tourists visiting your country. Tell them about:
— natural dangers such as strong sun, beaches with strong currents, or dangerous cliffs.
— their personal safety, and mention certain places where it is unwise to go alone or after sunset or without means of transport, e.g. a desert area.
— ways of looking after their personal property.
— special clothing for certain weather conditions, or as protection against wildlife or insects.
— areas of natural beauty that you think they should see.

Unit 7

Reading

Last summer, the Ingrams exchanged houses with some friends who live on the south coast of England. Joan Ingrams left a note to say where to find things.

Answer:

1. Where are the following:
   towels?
   extra blankets?
   vacuum cleaner?
   spare front door key?
   cat food?
   cat's bowl?
2. What does Joan ask Anne to do?
3. What instructions does she give about how much food to give the cat?

Writing

Imagine someone is going to stay in your home. Write a note to say where things are. Give any instructions or advice you think are necessary.

23/7

Just a short note to say where things are in the house. The sheets and towels are in the cupboard at the top of the stairs. Extra blankets are in the yellow wardrobe in the small bedroom.

The vacuum cleaner is in the cupboard under the stairs. There's a spare front door key on the shelf above the sink in the kitchen.

One more thing. Could you feed the cats?* Don't feed them more than once a day as they're on a diet! Also could you give them some water in their bowl outside the back door every day? Don't give them milk — they don't like it!

Hope you have a good time.

Love, Joan.

* The cat food is in the small cupboard under the sink in the kitchen.

Oral exercises

1. Confirm that you've got things
Have you got any eggs?
Oh, yes, lots of eggs.
Have you got any butter?
Oh, yes, lots of butter.

1. eggs?
2. butter?
3. onions?
4. cheese?
5. bread?
6. potatoes?

2. Say what you have and haven't got.
Look at the kitchen list on page 49.
Now, we need some onions and tomatoes.
*Well, there are some onions, but we haven't got
any tomatoes.*
What about milk and eggs?
Well, there is some milk, but we haven't got any eggs.

1. some onions and tomatoes
2. milk and eggs?
3. butter and fish
4. bread and meat?
5. yoghurt and apples

3. Ask what people have got (Open exercise)
You are staying with a friend for the weekend. Think
about what you would like to eat and ask your friend
if he has got any.

Now what would you like for breakfast?
Have you got any (eggs)?
Yes, sure. And what would you like with your coffee?
Have you got any (chocolate biscuits)?

1. Now what would you like for breakfast?
2. Yes, sure. And what would you like with your
   coffee?
3. No, I haven't. I'll get some for you. What about
   lunch? What would you like?
4. I think so. I'll have a look in the fridge. What
   would you like to drink with your lunch?
5. Yes, I have. And what would you like to have for
   tea?
6. No, I haven't. I'll go to the supermarket. Finally,
   there's supper. Is there anything special you would
   like?

4. Say where things are exactly
Look at the cupboards and drawers on page 49.

Where's the mayonnaise?
In the small cupboard on the top shelf.
Where are the kitchen knives?
In the middle drawer.

1. mayonnaise?
2. kitchen knives?
3. coffee?
4. cups and saucers?
5. flour?
6. bowls?

5. Ask people to do things in different ways
Repeat these sentences.
1. Give me a lift to the station, Rod.
2. Can you give me a lift to the station, Rod?
3. Could you give me a lift to the station, please, Rod?
4. Could you possibly give me a lift to the station,
   please, Rod?
Which request is least polite?
Which request is most polite?

6. Give warnings
A friend is planning a trip. You don't think his plans
are very sensible.
I'm going in the middle of August.
*Oh, don't go in the middle of August. That's not a good
idea.*
I'm driving, too.
Oh, don't drive. That's not a good idea.

1. I'm going in the middle of August.
2. I'm driving, too.
3. And I'm leaving on Friday evening.
4. I'm taking the children, too.
5. I'm driving all night.
6. I think I'll go through Central London.

Extra work
Re-express the warnings, like this:
1. *Oh, you shouldn't go in the middle of August.
   That's not a good idea.*

Unit 8　Excuses

🔲 **Dialogue　Part 1**

Lynne, a secretary who works in the same office as Rod, has family problems. Rod invites her round to his flat one evening to talk about them.

He is expecting her to arrive soon. Suddenly the telephone rings. He goes to answer it.

BARBARA:　Hello, Rod! Barbara here.
ROD:　　　Oh. Oh, hello, Barbara.
BARBARA:　Er... are you busy?
ROD:　　　Well, yes, actually. I'm just having a shower.
BARBARA:　Oh, sorry. I'll ring back later. OK?
ROD:　　　Er... yes. Fine. Bye!

Answer:
1. Where does Lynne work?
2. Why does Lynne want to talk to Rod?
3. Is Lynne there when the telephone rings?

Set 1 Interrupted activities

1. What's he doing? He's playing records.
What are they doing? They're entertaining
friends.

**Work in pairs. Match the pictures with the actions.
Ask and answer like this:**
What are the people in Picture 1 doing?
They're entertaining friends.
What's the **man** in Picture 2 doing?
He's listening to records.

Choose from these actions:

doing the housework
relaxing on the sofa
reading
feeding the baby
having a shower
painting the kitchen
putting the children to bed

washing her hair
making lunch
reading to the children
entertaining friends
playing records

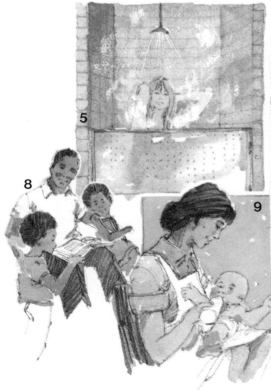

2. What are you doing? I'm playing records
with Pia.

**Work in pairs. Ask and answer about the pictures
in the same way.**

3. Write down what the people in the photographs are doing.

Carol is..................................

Tony is..................................

Barbara is..................................

The Coopers are ....

Joan Ingrams is ....

Lynne is ....

4. Are you busy? Am I { ringing at a bad time?
                            { disturbing you?
Well, yes, actually. I'm just having a shower.
No, I'm watching TV, but that's all right.

Rod and Jack are ....

Work in pairs. Telephone and interrupt all the people in the pictures. Make conversations like this:

A: Hello, Carol. It's ... here. Are you busy?
B: Well, yes, actually. I'm just drying my hair.
A: Oh, sorry I disturbed you. I'll ring back later.

or

A: Hello, Jack. It's ... here. Am I ringing at a bad time?
B: No. We're just watching television, but that's all right. You're not disturbing us.
A: Oh, don't worry. I'll ring back later.

5. Look at the list of activities in Exercises 1 and 3. Choose three bad times for people to phone you, like this:

It's a bad time to phone me

I don't like people { interrupting } me { when I'm ...
                      { disturbing }   { when ...

Work in pairs. Look at the list again and ask and answer like this:

Do you mind people phoning you when you're (drying your hair)?
Yes, definitely./No, not really./Sometimes. It depends.

🔊 Dialogue Part 2

Barbara telephones Rod again half an hour later. Lynne is already there.

BARBARA: Rod? It's me, Barbara. Am I ringing at a bad time again?

ROD: No, no. That's all right. Is it something important?

BARBARA: No, not really. It's just...well, some American friends of mine are here for a few days and they wanted to go for a meal this evening. I thought maybe you'd like to come, too.

ROD: Well, that does sound fun, but...er...I'm afraid, I've got a bad headache, to tell you the truth, and...

BARBARA: Oh, have you? I *am* sorry. Why don't you take a couple of asprins and lie down for a bit? You'll be all right in half an hour.

ROD: Yes, I know, but it's not just the headache. I'm afraid I really ought to do my washing this evening and I've got to write home to my parents, too.

BARBARA: Oh, well, shall we come round for a coffee later on instead?

ROD: Actually, I'd like to go to bed early tonight for once.

BARBARA: Oh, all right. Some other time then.

ROD: Look, Barbara, I'll ring you at work some time tomorrow.

BARBARA: Don't you remember? I'm leaving for Italy tomorrow.

ROD: Oh, yes. Of course. So you are. I remember now.

BARBARA: Well, have a nice evening, Rod.

ROD: Wait a minute, Barbara. I'll ring you early tomorrow morning and...

BARBARA: It's OK, Rod. I understand — perfectly. See you around.

Answer:

1. Is Rod alone in the flat when Barbara rings again?
2. Why does Barbara ring Rod?
3. Does Rod want to go? Why not?
4. What excuse does Rod make first?
5. What does Barbara suggest he does?
6. What is Rod's next excuse?
7. What does Barbara now suggest?
8. What is Rod's final excuse?
9. What do you think Barbara thinks?
10. Do you think Rod wants to see Barbara again?

Set 2 Invitations and acceptances

1. Look at the different invitations and find the following information:

1. What day of the week is the fiftieth birthday party?
2. What time does the children's birthday party start?
3. What is the name of the child giving it?
4. Where do Claire Andrews' parents live?
5. Where is the wedding reception to be held?
6. Is there a meal provided at the ICS anniversary party?

---

2. Would you like to
come to our party?

Yes, I'd love to.
That would be lovely.
Thank you.
Thank you. I'd like to come very much.

Use the invitations in the box below to invite each other to do things. Accept the invitations each time.

Would you like to ...

go out for a meal?
go to a disco?
go out for a walk?
go to the club?
go to the cinema?
come to a party?
come and play cards?
come round for a meal?
come to our Youth Club?
come and meet my friends?
Other things

....

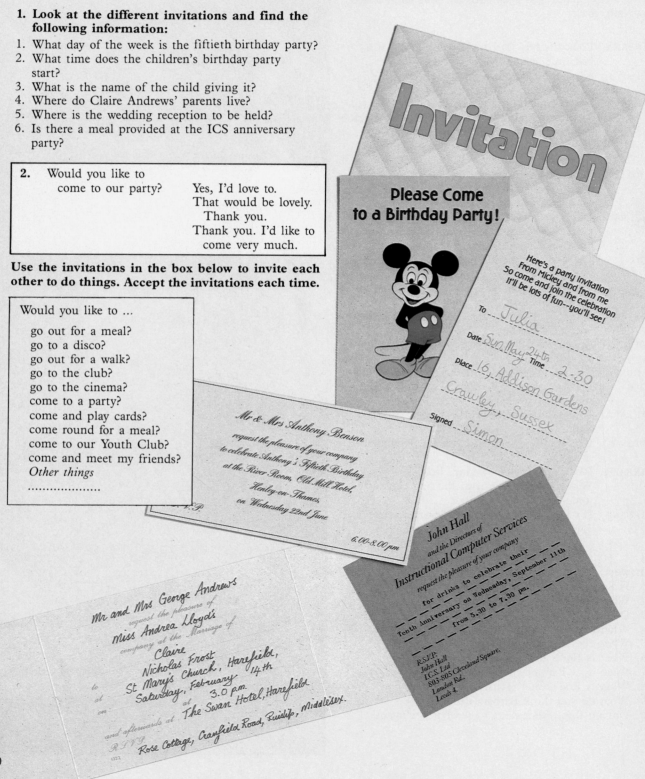

Invitation

Please Come to a Birthday Party!

Here's a party invitation
From Mickey and from me
So come and join the celebration
It'll be lots of fun--you'll see!

To _Julia_
Date _Sun May 24th_ Time _2·30_
Place _16, Addison Gardens_
Crawley, Sussex
Signed _Simon_

Mr & Mrs Anthony Benson
request the pleasure of your company
to celebrate Anthony's Fiftieth Birthday
at the River Room, Old Mill Hotel,
Henley-on-Thames,
on Wednesday 22nd June

R.V.P.

6.00-8.00 pm

John Hall
and the Directors of
Instructional Computer Services
request the pleasure of your company
for drinks to celebrate their
Tenth Anniversary on Wednesday, September 11th
from 5.30 to 7.30 pm.

R.S.V.P.
John Hall
I.C.S. Ltd
803-805 Cleveland Square,
London Rd.,
Leeds 4.

Mr and Mrs George Andrews
request the pleasure of
Miss Andrea Lloyd's
company at the Marriage of
Claire
to Nicholas Frost, Harefield,
at St Mary's Church, Harefield,
on Saturday, February 14th
at 3.0 p.m.
and afterwards at The Swan Hotel, Harefield
R.S.V.P.
Rose Cottage, Cranfield Road, Ruislip, Middlesex.

Set 3 Invitations, refusals and excuses

1. Would you like to come for a meal this evening?
Thanks very much. I'd love to, but I'm afraid
I ought to do my homework.

**Your partner invites you to do something; you
make an excuse, choosing from list number 1,
like this:**

A: Would you like to come to a party?
B: That's very kind of you, but I'm afraid I ought to
do my washing.
A: Oh, all right. Some other time then?
B: Yes, fine. Thanks for the invitation.

Thanks very much. I'd love to, but

1. I ought to do my washing.
get my things ready for work.
study for the class test.
....

2. I'd like to go to bed early.
write some letters.
make some phone calls.
wash my hair.
....

3. I've got to do some work.
I have to   do my homework.
go to a meeting.
wait for an important
phone call.
....

4. I've got a bad cold.
a bad headache.
a bad cough.
a sore throat.
....

2. Now choose excuses from the other three lists.

Roleplay
It is Sunday afternoon. You have nothing to do and are
bored. Telephone a friend. Work in pairs.

YOUR PARTNER   YOU

Answer the phone
and say your name.

Say who you are.

Greet your friend.

Ask if you are
disturbing your
friend.

Say you are not busy
and explain what
you are doing.

Invite your friend
to do something in
the evening.

Refuse the invitation
and make an excuse.

Repeat the same
invitation for
tomorrow evening.

Accept the invitation.

Say goodbye.

23 Oakfield Court,
Guildford Road,
Burton, Surrey

22nd February

Alison Merrit thanks Mr and Mrs James Hart for their kind invitation to their party on Saturday, March 6th, and has much pleasure in accepting.

Hill House Farm,
Burton, Surrey
22nd. Feb.

Dear James and Caroline,

Thank you so much for the invitation to your party on March 6th. John and I would love to come. It seems such a long time since we last saw you both.

We're looking forward to it very much.

Love,
Anna and John

... because of a previous engagement.

... owing to pressure of work.

... due to family commitments

... is unfortunately ill in hospital

Reading

Read this party invitation and a formal and informal letter of acceptance.

Mr and Mrs James Hart
will be
AT HOME
on Saturday March 6th
from 6.30 – 9.00 p.m.
R.S.V.P. 4 Purley Road, Burton, Surrey Tel: 253 6774

Answer:
1. Who is giving the party?
2. When is it?
3. Where is it at?
4. When does it start?
5. Are Anna and John looking forward to the party?
6. Who is the first letter to?
7. Who is it from?
8. What is unusual about it?
9. Do Anna and John see the Harts often?

Listening

Mr and Mrs Hart also received letters of *refusal* of the invitation to their party. Look at the last lines of four of them. Each gives the reason why various people cannot accept the Harts' invitation.

Each of the people also telephoned to explain personally why they couldn't come to the party. Match each telephone conversation (1, 2, 3 or 4) with the right letter by putting a number 1, 2, 3 or 4 against it.

Writing

1. Write a letter of invitation to your birthday party to a friend or partner. Give the time, date and place of the party (either at home or in a restaurant). Exchange the letters of invitation.

2. Write letters of acceptance or refusal as you wish, giving excuses where necessary.

1. Ask people to ring you back and give a reason
  (Open exercise)
Different people telephone you. You are busy.

Hello! It's Barbara here. Are you busy?
Well, actually, I'm (having supper) now. Could you ring me back later, Barbara?
Hi! This is Rod. Am I ringing at a bad time?
Well, actually, I'm (studying) now. Could you ring me back later, Rod?

1. Hello! It's Barbara here. Are you busy?
2. Hi! This is Rod. Am I ringing at a bad time?
3. Hello. This is Jack, Jack Cooper. Is this a good time to talk to you?
4. Hello. It's Joan here. Are you busy?
5. Good afternoon. This is Beautiful Homes Limited. Have you got a moment to spare?

2. Confirm excuses
You are working in an office. You explain to your boss why you and the others want to leave work early.

What's your excuse this time? A headache?
Yes. I have got a very bad headache.
What's the matter with Helen? A cold, I suppose.
Yes, she has got a very bad cold.

1. you/headache
2. Helen/a cold
3. Richard/pain in his shoulder
4. Carol/headache
5. Jan/pain in her back
6. you/cough

3. Invite people to do things (Open exercise)
Try to persuade some friends to go out with you.

Oh, dear. I've got to write some letters.
Really? Wouldn't you like to (go out for a meal) instead?
No, I ought to wash my hair.
Really? Wouldn't you like to (go out for a drink) instead?

1. write some letters
2. wash my hair
3. get ready for tomorrow
4. write some letters
5. study
6. do the washing

4. Repeat excuses
A friend tries to persuade you to go out. You don't want to go.

Oh, come on! One late night is all right. Let's go out.
I'd love to, but I really would like to go to bed early tonight.
We'll have a really great time. You can wash your hair tomorrow night.
I'd love to, but I really would like to wash my hair tonight.

1. Oh, come on! One late night is all right. Let's go out.
2. We'll have a really great time. You can wash your hair tomorrow night.
3. You can write some letters tomorrow. Why don't you come to the disco with us?
4. Come to the cinema with us — you can watch TV any time.
5. Oh, do let's go out. You can do the washing on Sunday.
6. You need to go out more. You can work tomorrow.

5. Make excuses (Open exercise)
Make your own excuses to a friend.

Couldn't I come round for a chat?
Sorry, but (I ought to do some washing).
But what about later?
Sorry, but (I'd like to go to bed early).

1. Couldn't I come round for a chat?
2. But what about later?
3. Shall we do something exciting this evening?
4. But what about having a meal together? I know — you could come round here.
5. All right. But couldn't I come round just for a few minutes — just for a chat — you know?
6. What about tomorrow evening then?

Extra work
Re-express the excuses, like this:
1. *Sorry, but I have to do my washing.*

Unit 9 Future plans

People in Business ... *IN BRISTOL*

A pretty future for pretty feet

This month's Bristol Business Personality is in the retail trade. She is Barbara Cooper, manageress of the shoe boutique called 'Pretty Feet'.

Professional person
My appointment with Ms Cooper was for afternoon tea on Sunday. 'I'm afraid I can't see you at any other time,' she said when I phoned her during the week at her boutique. 'Are you sure that you don't mind giving up some of your free time?' I enquired. 'Oh, not at all,' she replied. 'After all, I am a professional person and any publicity is good publicity.'

So I took the lift to the sixth floor of a brand new apartment block with a view of the River Avon and joined Barbara Cooper for tea. As she sat in her light and airy sitting room on a comfortable sofa, I noticed her bare feet. She laughed and said, 'I like selling shoes, but I don't like wearing them much. I always take them off when I get home!'

Remarkable success
Still only in her mid-twenties, Barbara Cooper is already a remarkable success. From starting work as an assistant in a second-hand clothes shop, she is now the manageress of a fashionable shoe shop called 'Pretty Feet'.

All over Europe
'We sell shoes,' she said, 'to all sorts of people — young and old. But the younger end of the market doesn't like wearing mass-produced British shoes. Therefore I've got to travel abroad a lot. I buy lots of different designs from all over Europe.' She makes about six trips abroad every year on average to find new products. 'People now want a wide range of choice as well as high-quality shoes,' she says. Next week she is going to fly to Milan to look at some of the new season's Italian designs.

Future plans
And what are her plans for the future? Barbara explained, 'We're going to open branches of 'Pretty Feet' in other cities — first London, then Manchester and Birmingham, and after that, Leeds. Then we'll make decisions about whether to develop internationally or not.' She laughed again. 'This year Leeds, next year Los Angeles. We'll have to see how things go.'

We finished our tea and she showed me to the door. 'Come along and see us in the shop one day,' she said, and then added, 'Remember we sell shoes to all sorts of people!'

Obviously things are going to turn out pretty well for Barbara Cooper.

Next month: Paul and Linda Gerrard — King and Queen of the Pizza Palaces

1. Answer:
1. What is Barbara's flat like?
2. Where was Barbara sitting?
3. Was Barbara wearing shoes?
4. What was Barbara's first job?
5. What does she do now?
6. Why does Barbara buy lots of different designs from abroad?
7. How often does Barbara travel abroad?
8. What are Barbara's plans for next week?
9. What are her plans for the future?
10. What does the reporter think of Barbara's future?
11. Do you think the reporter was young?
12. Do you think Barbara's last remark was rude or amusing?

2. Find words in the text which mean the opposite of:

amateur	put on	new
answered	failure	old-fashioned
dark		hand-made

3. Write questions for these answers:
1. It's light and airy.
2. No, she wasn't. She had bare feet.
3. On a sofa.
4. Between twenty and thirty.
5. An assistant in a local second-hand clothes shop.
6. To buy different designs for the younger market.
7. About six times a year.
8. To Italy.
9. To open branches in London, Manchester, Birmingham and Leeds.

4. Correct these statements:
1. Barbara lives in a house in Bristol.
2. She sat on a chair during the interview.
3. She and the reporter drank coffee.
4. Barbara is over thirty.
5. She is a shop assistant in a local shoeshop.
6. She travels to Italy about six times a year.
7. There are branches of the shoe boutique in London, Manchester and Birmingham.

Set 1 Plans

1. Where are you going to go? *or* Where are you going? How are you going to travel? Where are you going to stay? How long are you going to spend there? What are you going to do there?	To Italy. By car. At a hotel. A week. Sightsee.	Really? How lovely! Oh, yes? That sounds fun.

Work in pairs. Imagine you are:

either a family with two children, aged 12 and 8
or a young couple without children
or a couple of students.

Decide what you are going to do on your next summer holiday. Make notes. Use the holiday plans below to help you.

	HOLIDAY PLANS	
1.	Where are you going to go? *or* Where are you going?	To the USA Italy Japan Bali
2.	How are you going to travel?	By plane (air) boat (sea) train car boat and train
3.	Where are you going to stay?	At a hotel guest house youth hostel camping site In a Bed and Breakfast place With friends With relations
4.	How long are you going to spend there?	A week A fortnight Three weeks A month
5.	What are you going to do there?	Sightsee Swim and lie on the beach Visit friends Go walking and climbing Travel round the country

2. Ask other pairs about their plans.

Roleplay

Your partner is going on holiday. He/she plans to spend three weeks in a small hotel in Rome. Talk to your partner about his/her holiday.

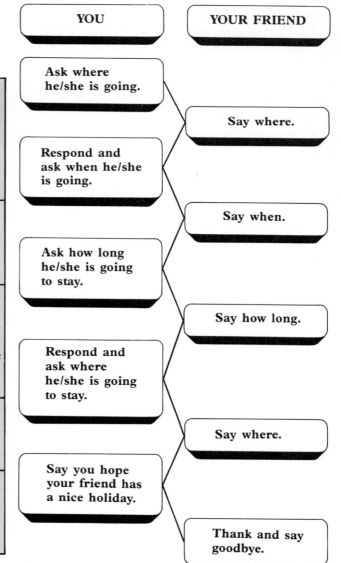

YOU

Ask where he/she is going.

Respond and ask when he/she is going.

Ask how long he/she is going to stay.

Respond and ask where he/she is going to stay.

Say you hope your friend has a nice holiday.

YOUR FRIEND

Say where.

Say when.

Say how long.

Say where.

Thank and say goodbye.

Dialogue

Before Barbara left for Italy, she talked to her shop assistant, Gerry, about her plans, and reminded him to look after everything when she was away.

BARBARA: Gerry, I'm going to leave for the airport in half an hour. Can I have a word with you first?

GERRY: Yes, sure. How long are you going to spend in Italy, by the way?

BARBARA: Oh, just a week. I'm going to see some new designers this time, so it will be quite interesting. Now — you'll remember to check the till every evening, won't you?

GERRY: Yes, I will. Don't worry.

BARBARA: And you won't forget to lock all the doors when you leave?

GERRY: No, I won't. Relax, Barbara.

BARBARA: OK. Well, I must get ready. Oh, has Rod phoned this morning?

GERRY: No.

BARBARA: Oh. Oh, well. Look at the weather. It's going to rain again.

GERRY: What's the weather like in Italy at this time of year?

BARBARA: They say it's quite warm and sunny.

GERRY: Lucky you!

BARBARA: Gerry, don't forget I'm not going to have a holiday. I'm going there to work! Now, I think I ought to call a taxi...

Answer:
1. When did Barbara talk to Gerry?
2. When is she going to leave for Italy?
3. What are her plans?
4. What does she remind Gerry to do?
5. Is the weather good in Bristol?
6. What's the weather like in Italy?
7. Is Barbara going to have a holiday in Italy?

| **1.** Barbara talked to Gerry. Then she left for Italy. |
| = |
| Before Barbara left for Italy, she talked to Gerry. |

Link these sentences with Before.
1. She checked the till. Then she locked the shop.
2. She talked to Gerry. Then she telephoned for a taxi.
3. She telephoned her parents. Then she left for Italy.

| **2.** (The time is 9.00.) I'm going to leave at 9.30. |
| = |
| I'm going to leave *in* half an hour. |

Make sentences using in. **Imagine the time is 9.00 and you are going to leave at:**

9.10 I'm going to leave in ten minutes.
9.15
9.35
10.00
11.00

Set 2 Reminders

1. A: You'll remember to check the till, won't you?
B: Yes, I will. Don't worry.
A: You won't forget to lock all the doors, will you?
B: No, I won't. Don't worry.

A friend is going away on holiday. Remind him/her to do these things in the same way:
1. Lock front and back door
2. Close all windows
3. Turn off lights
4. Turn off electric fires and fridge
5. Cancel newspapers
6. Tell police you are going away

Like this:
You'll remember to lock the front and back door, won't you?
Yes, I will. Don't worry.
And you won't forget to ..., will you?
No, I won't. Don't worry.

2. Match these reminders with the pictures on the right.
1. Don't forget to lock your car doors!
2. Remember to cancel your newspapers when you go away on holiday!
3. Remember to look both ways when you cross the road!
4. Don't forget to fasten your seat belt!
5. Don't forget to check your passport before you go on holiday!

3. How would you remind a friend who is:
1. going on a long car journey?
   (check ... take ...)
2. going to leave his house for 3 months?
   (lock ... tell ... turn off ... cancel ...)
3. going for an interview for a job?
   (be ... wear ... answer ... ask ...)
4. going to take some children on a long train journey?
   (take ... wear ... buy ... eat ... drink ...)

Practise short conversations in pairs.

Unit 9

Set 3 Weather

1. **Match the weather words and phrases below with the pictures.**

cloudy	it's stormy
windy	it's raining
cold and foggy	it's snowing
hot and sunny	it's freezing

2. **Say what the weather is like in your area today.**

3. What's the weather like in Amsterdam?
   Miserable! It's raining and cold.
   What's the weather like in Malaga?
   Lovely! It's sunny and quite hot.

Work in pairs. Look at the chart.
Ask and answer about:

the capital of Greece
two cities in Italy
a city in Canada
a capital city in Scandinavia

two cities in Britain
the capital of Yugoslavia
a city in Spain
a city in Germany

World Weather AT NOON YESTERDAY

	C	F			C	F			C	F			C	F
Amstrdm	R	10 50	Berlin	C	14 57	Cardiff	C	13 55	Geneva	C	12 54
Athens	S	19 66	Bermuda	S	24 75	Cologne	C	10 50	Gibraltar	S	20 68
Barcelona	F	19 66	Biarritz	S	16 61	Copenhgn	C	9 48	Glasgow	C	12 54
Beirut	S	25 77	Bristol	C	13 55	Dublin	F	12 54	Guernsey	C	11 52
Belfast	C	11 52	Brussels	C	11 52	Edinburgh	F	10 50	Helsinki	R	9 48
Belgrade	S	15 59	Budapest	F	15 59	Florence	F	17 63	Jersey	C	13 55
L Palmas	S	20 68	Malta	F	18 64	Nice	S	17 63	Toronto	C	13 55
Lisbon	C	18 64	Manchstr	C	13 55	Oslo	C	12 54	Tunis	F	21 70
London	R	11 52	Moscow	F	13 55	Paris	C	13 55	Vancouvr	R	10 50
							Rome	S	18 64	Venice	C	14 57
Madrid	S	23 73	Munich	R	12 54	Stockholm	C	6 43	Vienna	F	15 59
Majorca	S	19 66	Naples	F	17 63	Tel Aviv	S	23 73	Warsaw	F	14 57
Malaga	S	20 68	New York	C	11 52	Tenerife	F	17 63	Zurich	F	13 55

C — cloud, F — fair, R — rain, S — sun, Sn — snow.

Reading

Letters to the Editor

Who's going to pay?

Sir,

Last night I watched a Party Political broadcast on television. It was on behalf of the present government and in it, the Prime Minister outlined the aims of the government. It made me very angry.

To be fair, their plans for the future of this country are certainly interesting. They say they are going to build more day nurseries for mothers who go out to work. They say they are going to build more schools and increase the grants of university and college students. Then they say they are going to reduce unemployment; improve the National Health Service; cut the cost of dental treatment. And they say they intend to reduce the level of personal taxation. In the same breath they say they are going to cut inflation and thereby reduce the cost of living and help family budgets. (Are you still with me?) Oh, yes, I nearly forgot. They are going to spend millions of pounds on a nuclear defence system to protect us from an enemy attack.

But the question I want to ask is: where are they going to get all the money to put their ideas into practice? Well, I think I know the answer. The money is going to come out of the taxpayer's pocket. That's right! It's you and me who are going to pay the bill.

Sir, may I suggest that the present state of the national economy means these plans are not only unrealistic, they're irresponsible and completely unbelievable.

    M. C. Downing (Ms)
    Stockley, Manchester.

Answer:

1. What are the government going to do about day nurseries?
2. What are they going to do about student grants?
3. What are they going to do about unemployment?
4. What about the National Health Service?
5. And what about taxation?
6. How are the government going to reduce the cost of living?
7. What are they going to do about defence?
8. What question does Ms Downing ask?
9. What is her answer?
10. What does she think of the government's plans?

Listening 1

Listen to these people talking about their holiday plans to some friends. Fill in the details.

	Jane	Elizabeth
Country/Place Transport Length of stay Accommodation Activities		

Now write two short paragraphs describing their plans like this:

Jane is going to ...

Listening 2

The Ingrams plan to spend a day by the seaside at Weston-super-Mare. Before they leave, they listen to the weather forecast for the day.

    Listen to the forecast and make notes about the weather. Then decide what activities would be best for the morning/at lunchtime/the afternoon, e.g. sunbathing? swimming? looking at the shops? having a picnic lunch? going to the cinema? going for a walk?

    What clothes should they take? Swimming things? Raincoats? Umbrellas?

Write them a short note with some advice about the day.

Writing

Write three or four paragraphs about your plans for your next long holiday. Say when and where you are going and what you hope to see and do.

Oral exercises

1. Ask about people's travel plans
I'm going to Italy next week.
Oh, are you? How long are you going to stay?
Rod's going to Canada next July.
Oh, is he? How long is he going to stay?

1. I/Italy/next week
2. Rod/Canada/next July
3. My daughter and her family/Spain/for a holiday
4. Paul/Germany/next month
5. Barbara/business trip/Milan

2. Ask about people's accommodation plans
I'm going to spend the summer in Greece.
Where are you going to stay? At a hotel?
We're going to Bournemouth.
Where are you going to stay? At a guest house?

1. I/spend the summer in Greece
2. We/Bournemouth
3. Lynne/central part of France
4. The Ingrams/Portugal by car
5. The Parkers/have three weeks in southern Spain
6. Barbara/have a cheap holiday in Scotland

3. Say what you are going to do or buy in different places (Open exercise)
What are you going to buy when you go to Italy?
I'm going to (buy some shoes).
Oh, that's nice.
What are you going to do when you go to the south of France?
I'm going to (swim and lie on the beach).
Oh, that sounds lovely.

1. What are you going to buy when you go to Italy?
2. What are you going to do when you go to the south of France?
3. What are you going to do when you go to New York?
4. What are you going to buy when you go to London?
5. What are you going to do when you go to Scotland?

4. Remind yourself to do things
You and your family are going away. You go through a list of reminders of things to do before you leave.

Remember the windows.
Yes, I won't forget to shut them.
Remember the door.
Yes, I won't forget to lock it.

1. the windows (shut)   4. the newspapers (cancel)
2. the door (lock)   5. the fridge (turn off)
3. the lights (turn off)

5. Reassure people
Don't forget to shut the windows.
No, don't worry. I won't.
You'll remember to lock the door, won't you?
Yes, don't worry. I will.

1. Don't forget to shut the windows.
2. You'll remember to lock the door, won't you?
3. Please don't forget to post my letters.
4. You will remember to phone me this evening, won't you?
5. Before you go away, don't forget to get some travellers' cheques.
6. Remember to buy me some stamps, won't you?

6. Ask what the weather is like in different countries
I'm going to France in April.
Oh yes, what's the weather like there in April?
Oh, it's sometimes quite warm, I think.
I'm going to Greece in February.
Oh yes, what's the weather like there in February?
Oh, it rains a lot.

1. France in April   4. Egypt in October
2. Greece in February   5. Scotland in March
3. Norway in the spring 6. Argentina in July

Turin • Milan
Florence
Rome
Naples
Adriatic Sea
Mediterranean Sea

🔊 **Dialogue**

Barbara Cooper is in Milan on a business trip. She is sitting in a small café outside the central station waiting to catch a train to Florence. Suddenly she sees an old school friend, Martha Hunt, walking past the café.

BARBARA: Martha!

MARTHA: Barbara!

BARBARA: What are you doing here? You live in Manchester, don't you?

MARTHA: Yes, that's right. I do. But I'm having a week's holiday here.

BARBARA: What? Here in Milan?

MARTHA: Yes, I'm visiting a friend. You know him actually — Roger.

BARBARA: Yes, I remember Roger.

MARTHA: Well, he's working here as a freelance journalist.

BARBARA: Is he? That must be fun.

MARTHA: Well, he says he's enjoying it. What about you? What are you doing here? Having a holiday as well?

BARBARA: No, not me. I'm working. I'm looking for some new shoe designs for the shop.

MARTHA: Oh, yes. I read about you in the Old Cliftonians' magazine. You're the manageress of a shoe shop now, aren't you?

BARBARA: Yes, that's right. It's doing quite well, in fact.

MARTHA: Which hotel are you staying at, by the way?

BARBARA: Well, I'm not staying in Milan any more. I'm catching the train to Florence in half an hour. In fact, I must go soon.

MARTHA: Oh, that's a pity. Anyway, I must go too. I must try and come and see you in Bristol one day.

BARBARA: Yes, do. And give my regards to Roger.

MARTHA: Yes, I will. Well — look after yourself and don't work too hard.

BARBARA: No, I won't. Have a nice holiday, by the way!

MARTHA: Thanks. Bye, Barbara!

Answer:
1. Why is Barbara in Milan?
2. Where is she sitting when she meets Martha?
3. Why is she sitting there?
4. Who is Martha?
5. Why is she in Italy?
6. Who is Roger?
7. Does Barbara know him?
8. Does Roger like his job as a freelance journalist?
9. What is Barbara doing in Milan?
10. How does Martha know that Barbara is the manageress of a shoe shop?
11. Does Barbara say her shoe shop is successful?
12. When is Barbara leaving for Florence?
13. How is she going to travel?
14. How many ways of saying goodbye can you find?

TEN YEARS ON:
What are you doing now?

A special feature for the Evening Post by Mike Sanders

Last week I was looking through old editions of the Bristol Evening Post. I found one copy which was ten years old. In it was a class photograph of the fifth form at Clifton Park Comprehensive School. I looked at those bright young faces and thought, "I wonder what they are doing now?"

So I decided to do some research. Look below and see what I discovered.

Name:	Barbara Cooper	Martha Hunt	John Murphy
Now lives in:	Bristol	Manchester	Aberdeen
Job:	Manageress of shoe shop in Bristol	Doctor at Manchester General Hospital	Engineer for an American Oil Company
Other news:	Barbara is studying shoe design at Bristol Technical College.	Martha is hoping to become an Ear, Nose and Throat specialist.	At the moment, John is working on an oil rig in the North Sea.

Name:	Terry Fisher	James Black	Clive Parker
Now lives in:	Birmingham	London	Madrid
Job:	Carpenter for a small building firm	Librarian at the North East London Polytechnic	English Language teacher in a large school in Madrid
Other news:	Terry is looking for a job in the car industry.	James is studying for a sociology degree.	Clive and his wife are expecting their first child.

1. Roleplay two meetings:
between Barbara and John.
between Martha and Clive.

Find out about each other's news. Start your conversations like this:

JOHN: Where are you living now, Barbara?
BARBARA: In Bristol. I'm the manageress of a shoe shop there.
JOHN: Oh, are you? Do you like the job?
BARBARA: Oh, yes. And I'm also studying shoe design at Bristol Technical College.
JOHN: That sounds interesting.
BARBARA: And what about you, John? Where are you living now?
JOHN: ....

2. Work in pairs. Ask and answer about the people in the article, like this:

Do you know where ... is living now?
Yes. I think he's/she's ...
What is he/she doing now?
He's/She's ...
Do you know any other news about him/her?
Yes. I think he's/she's ...

3. Work in pairs. Ask and tell each other details about your own personal news.

4. Read the paragraph below, then write a similar paragraph for Martha, John, Terry, James and Clive.

Barbara Cooper is now living in Bristol where she is the manageress of a shoe shop. In her spare time she is studying shoe design at Bristol Technical College.

Roleplay

You are in the street and you see a friend you haven't met for some time.

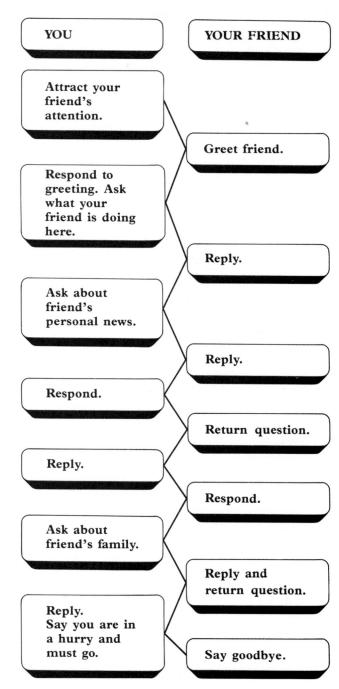

YOU	YOUR FRIEND
Attract your friend's attention.	
	Greet friend.
Respond to greeting. Ask what your friend is doing here.	
	Reply.
Ask about friend's personal news.	
	Reply.
Respond.	
	Return question.
Reply.	
	Respond.
Ask about friend's family.	
	Reply and return question.
Reply. Say you are in a hurry and must go.	
	Say goodbye.

Set 2 Confirmation and correction

1. Your name's Barbara Cooper, isn't it?	Yes, that's right.
You live in Bristol, don't you?	That's right, I do.
And you're the manageress of a shoe shop, aren't you?	Yes, I am. That's right.
You're studying for a degree in sociology, aren't you?	No. I'm studying shoe design.

Roleplay an interview. You are Mike Sanders, the newspaper reporter.
Your partner is one of the people on page 74.
Check certain facts about his/her present life. Your partner must
confirm or correct the facts, like this:

Your name is Martha Hunt, isn't it?   Yes, ...
And you live in Bristol, don't you?   No, I ...
Oh, yes. Sorry. But you're a doctor, aren't you? Yes, I ...

Ask and answer in the same way about each person.

2. Think about your partner or friend in your class. Write down
**   five facts about him/her that you know or believe are true,**
**   e.g. his/her name, where he/she lives, his/her job, interests,**
**   etc. Then check your facts with your partner, like this:**

Your name is ..., isn't it?
You live in ..., don't you?
You're a ..., aren't you?

3. Leningrad is a city in the Soviet Union, isn't it?	That's right, it is.
Milan is by the sea, isn't it?	No, it isn't actually.
Britain has got breakfast-time TV, hasn't it?	That's right, it has.
Britain has still got compulsory military service, hasn't it?	No, it hasn't, actually.
Queen Christina was Swedish, wasn't she?	That's right, she was.
El Greco was an Italian artist, wasn't he?	No, he wasn't, actually.
The Beatles were an English pop group, weren't they?	That's right, they were.
The Ancient Romans were Christians, weren't they?	No, they weren't.
El Greco, the artist, lived in Toledo in Spain, didn't he?	That's right, he did.
The Ancient Greeks believed in God, didn't they?	No, they didn't, actually.

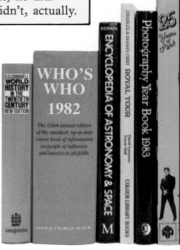

In pairs, ask for confirmation of statements in the same way.
 1. The police in Britain always carry guns.
 2. Scotland is famous for its scenery.
 3. The River Thames flows through Bristol.
 4. In Britain, motorists drive on the left-hand side of the road.
 5. Napoleon was a Russian General.
 6. Ingrid Bergman was a Swedish actress.
 7. The Americans were the first people to land on the moon.
 8. Captain Cook discovered America.
 9. The Chinese invented acupuncture.
10. Amy Johnson flew solo from London to Australia.

4. Make a list of six or more similar enquiries concerning countries,
**   famous people or general knowledge of the world. Make some**
**   of them true and some of them false and ask your partner**
**   to confirm or correct them.**

Set 3 Farewells and greetings

A	B
I really must go now. Look, I must go now. Heavens! Look at the time — I must rush, I'm afraid.	Yes, I must go, too. Yes, I'm in a bit of a hurry, too.
Give my regards to Joe. Give my love to your parents. Look after yourself! Have a nice time/weekend/holiday! Enjoy yourself! Be good! Come and see us some time.	Yes, I will. Thanks. I will.
Don't work too hard. Don't forget to write. Don't drive too fast. Don't forget to phone me.	No, I won't.
Don't do anything I wouldn't do!	No. Don't worry. I won't.
Have a nice weekend. Have a lovely Christmas! Merry Christmas! Happy New Year! Happy Easter!	Thanks. And to you!
Bye! See you! Goodbye! See you soon, I hope. Bye! See you on Monday!	Yes, I hope so. Yes. See you soon! Yes. Bye!
Goodbye! It was nice meeting you.	Yes. I hope we meet again some time. Goodbye!

Work in pairs. Practise making and responding to parting remarks, using the tables. You read out a parting remark from column A; then your partner chooses a suitable response from column B, like this:

I really must go now.
Yes, I'm in a bit of a hurry, too.

Unit 10

🔊 **Listening**

Listen to some international scientists talking about their present research activitites. Fill in the chart with the correct information.

	Dr Pierre Chabrol	Dr Brian Powers	Dr Carmen Hernandez
Subject:			
Place:			
University:			

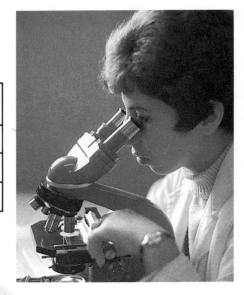

Now write a short paragraph about one of the scientists for a scientific journal. Start like this:
Dr Chabrol is at present investigating ...

Reading
Read the letter which Peggy Cooper wrote to her sister who emigrated to New Zealand just after the war.

Air Mail

Stella Barclay
33, Park Road
Christchurch
New Zealand

1. Answer:
What news do you learn about the following:
Stella?   Peggy?
Jack?   the situation at
Barbara?   Western?

2. Look up the words and expressions in a dictionary and use them in sentences of your own.

1. up to date
2. work overtime
3. ups and downs
4. wage claim
5. mixed feelings
6. settle down

Writing
Write a letter to an old friend of your family. Give news about yourself and other members of the family. Don't forget to ask for news about your friend and his/her family.

8 Belmont Crescent,
Bristol 9.

April 11th

Dear Stella,

Thank you very much for your long letter. It was lovely to hear all your news and get up to date. Please forgive me for not writing sooner, but I have been terribly busy at work. (I worked overtime all last week.) I was sorry to hear about your illness. I hope you are getting proper treatment.

We are having our ups and downs here, too. Jack is still Production Manager at Western. He's working extremely hard at the moment on an important order for France. He always seems tired when he comes home at night. Unfortunately, things aren't going too well at Western. There's a lot of trouble over wage claims and Jack thinks that there's probably going to be a strike. Jack has mixed feelings about the situation, but between you and me, I think he's getting tired of it all. In fact, he's thinking of putting in an application to join the project which Western are setting up on the Continent. It's in Toulouse in the south-west part of France - do you remember we went there when we were children? We are still discussing whether to go or not. In a way I don't really want to move away from all my friends here, but I realise that we ought to think seriously about it.

Barbara isn't living at home any more. She's got a flat of her own. Her shop is doing well and she travels abroad a lot. She's away in Italy at the moment. (I enclose a cutting about Barbara from the local paper. They chose her as "Business Personality of the Month" !) She's got a new boyfriend who works at Western with Jack. He's very nice - Canadian - but I don't think it's a very serious relationship. You know what Barbara is like. She never has been keen to settle down.

Well, that seems to be all my news at the moment. I'm going to try and catch the last post, so I'll stop now.

All the best from us both.

Love,
Peggy

78

Oral exercises

1. Answer questions about people's lives

Do you know where Barbara's living now?
Yes, in Bristol.
Do you know what Martha's doing now?
Yes, she's a doctor in Manchester General Hospital.

1. Barbara/live?
2. Martha/do?
3. John Murphy/live?
4. Terry/do?
5. James/live?
6. Clive Parker/do?

2. Correct information about people's lives

Barbara's living in Manchester, isn't she?
No, no, not Manchester. Bristol.
John's working in London, isn't he?
No, no, not London. Aberdeen.

1. Barbara/live/Manchester?
2. John/work/London?
3. Terry/work/Liverpool?
4. Martha/live/Bristol?
5. James/work/Scotland?
6. Clive/live/Mexico?

3. Ask for precise information about people's lives

Terry Fisher has got a job with a building firm.
Really! What exactly is he doing?
He's a carpenter, I think.
The Parkers are living in Spain.
Really! Where exactly are they living?
In Madrid, as far as I know.
1. Terry Fisher's got a job with a building firm.
2 The Parkers are living in Spain.
3. Paul's studying at the Polytechnic.
4. John's working for an oil company.
5. Terry and his wife are living in the Midlands.
6. Martha's working in a hospital.

Extra work

Re-express the statements like this:
1. *Terry Fisher has got a job with a bulding firm, hasn't he?*

4. Express surprise about people's lives

I'm working on an oil rig.
Oh, are you?
And my sister's living in America now.
Oh, is she?
Yes, and she likes it. But it's a long way from
my parents. You see, they're living in France at
the moment.
Oh, are they?

1. I/work/on an oil rig
2. My sister/live/in America
3. My parents/live/in/France at the moment
4. James/study/for a degree at present
5. Clive/work/in Madrid now
6. He and his wife/expect/their first child

5. Confirm and correct facts about people and places

Barbara works in a shoe shop, doesn't she?
That's right, she does.
The shop's in the centre of Bristol, isn't it?
That's right, it is.
Rod works in a car factory, doesn't he?
*No, he doesn't, actually. He works at Western
Aeronautics.*

1. Barbara/work/shoe shop?
2. Shop/be/in the centre of Bristol?
3. Rod/work/in a car factory?
4. He/work/with Jack Cooper?
5. Barbara/be/Jack Cooper's daughter?
6. Barbara/live/at home with her parents?

6. Say goodbye in different ways (Open
   exercise)

Say goodbye to these people in the way you think best.

ROD: See you on Monday! Bye!
        (Yes. Bye!)
PEGGY: Goodbye, and have a lovely weekend!
        (Thanks and the same to you.)

1. See you on Monday! Bye!
2. Goodbye, and have a lovely weekend!
3. Cheerio! And enjoy yourself tonight!
4. I really must go now. Cheerio!
5. Bye! And don't forget to send me a postcard!
6. Have a good trip and look after yourself!

Unit 11 Consolidation

❶ Read and complete these conversations.

1. A: I'm going to Greece for a week in May.
   B: ....?
   A: They say it's quite warm, but not really warm enough to swim.

2. A: ....?
   B: This afternoon? I'm going to stay at home and work in the garden.

3. A: ....?
   B: I'm afraid I'm a non-smoker. I don't like the smell of tobacco at all.

4. A: ....?
   B: No, we finished all the eggs yesterday.

5. A: What have we got in the fridge?
   B: .... That's all.
   C: Oh, well, let's have a cheese omelette then.

6. A: ....
   B: No, don't worry. I won't. I always lock it when I leave.

7. A: Would you like to go out for a walk with us?
   B: ....
   A: Oh, have you? I *am* sorry. Why don't you take an aspirin and lie down?

8. A: Do you feel like going out this evening?
   B: ....
   A: But your hair looks all right to me.

9. A: Am I ringing at a bad time?
   B: ....
   A: Are you sure? I can phone back when the programme is over if you like.

10. A: ....?
    B: Sally Fisher? Oh, she's working as a lawyer for a large organisation in Singapore.
    A: ....?
    B: For about six months, I think.

11. A: New York is the capital of the United States of America, isn't it?
    B: ....

12. A: ....
    B: I know, but I want to get a really good suntan.

❷ A special dinner

You are going to cook a special dinner this evening. In your fridge and food cupboard at home there is:

chicken stock	flour	pepper
onions	rice	oranges
butter	salt	cheese

CHICKEN BLANQUETTE

1 chicken
1 onion
250gm mushrooms
100gm butter
½ litre of chicken stock
100gm flour
2—3 tablespoons cream
a few drops of lemon juice
salt and pepper

This is your dinner menu:

Prawn Cocktail
Chicken Blanquette
Green Salad ~ Courgettes ~ rice
Strawberries and Cream

Work in pairs. One of you makes a list of all the food you will need to prepare the dinner. The other has the list of food that you have already got in the house. Ask and answer like this:
Have we got any prawns?
No, we haven't.
Oh, well let's get some prawns then.

Make a list of all the things you need to buy. Then read your list out like this:
We need some ..., a ..., some ... and some ....

3

1. Where does all the money go?
In pairs, find out which items in this weekly budget are appropriate to your situation. Then make a budget which applies to you.

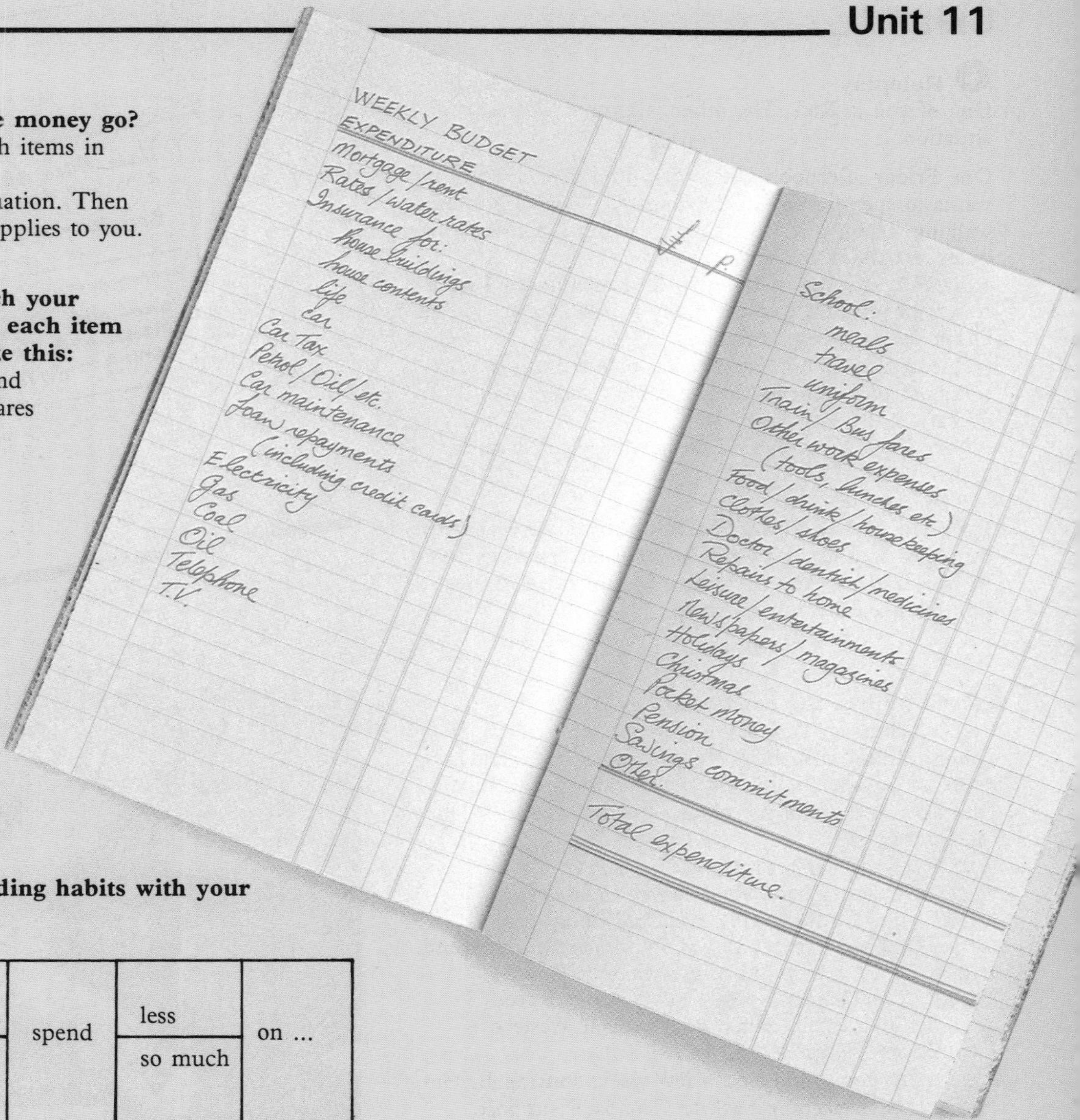

2. Find out how much your partner spends on each item on the list. Ask like this:
How much do you spend approximately on bus fares each week?

WEEKLY BUDGET
EXPENDITURE

£ p

Mortgage/rent
Rates/water rates
Insurance for:
   House buildings
   house contents
   Life
   Car
Car Tax
Petrol/Oil/etc.
Car maintenance
Loan repayments
   (including credit cards)
Electricity
Gas
Coal
Oil
Telephone
T.V.

School:
   meals
   travel
   uniform
Train/Bus fares
Other work expenses
   (tools, lunches etc.)
Food/drink/housekeeping
Clothes/shoes
Doctor/dentist/medicines
Repairs to home
Leisure/entertainments
Newspapers/magazines
Holidays
Christmas
Pocket money
Pension
Savings commitments
Other

Total expenditure.

3. Discuss your spending habits with your partner, like this:

I	should ought to	spend	less	on ...
	shouldn't oughtn't to don't have to		so much	

4 **Most accidents with small children happen in the home. What advice or instructions can you give to parents of small children? Make as many sentences as you can from the chart below.**

Remember to Always Don't forget to You should	put away keep them away from	matches. sharp knives (after using them). scissors (after using them). electrical equipment when it's on. plugs and sockets. boiling water.
You shouldn't Never You should never	let them touch let them go near let them play with	fires when they're on. the iron when it's on. the cooker when it's on.

Unit 11

❺ Roleplay

One of you is Rod. The other is Lynne. This is the situation:

One Friday afternoon after work, Rod decides that he wants to spend a day in the country — driving around, walking, seeing the local sights, having lunch in a nice, quiet restaurant and so on.

Barbara is away in Italy, so Rod telephones Lynne to ask her to join him for a day in the country — either on Saturday or Sunday.

But in fact, Lynne has already planned to do other things at the weekend, so she cannot accept his invitation.

Now look at the page from her diary for Saturday and Sunday.

Prepare and then act the telephone conversation between Lynne and Rod. Rod must try very hard to persuade Lynne to come. Lynne must make her excuses for not coming.

❻ Complete the conversation.

Rod is talking to Paul, his flat-mate, one Friday evening. They talk about Paul's studies and what he is going to do after he has finished at the polytechnic. Paul asks Rod about his plans — and Barbara's — for the future.

ROD: ....? *(What/read)*

PAUL: Oh, it's a book about naval engineering.

ROD: .... on a Friday evening? *(Why/read)*

PAUL: Because I've got to write an essay this weekend.

ROD: .... when you're qualified? *(What/do)*

PAUL: I don't know. I'd like to get a job abroad, I think. .... when your year at Western is over? *(What/do)*

ROD: I'm going to spend a few weeks touring Britain, then I'm going back to Canada, I suppose.

PAUL: .... *(What/Barbara/do)*

ROD: I think she's going to open a branch of 'Pretty Feet' in London.

PAUL: .... in Italy? *(What/she/do)*

ROD: She's seeing some designers there. She's coming back tomorrow. By the way, ... on Saturday evening? *(What/you and Sue/do)*

PAUL: I don't know yet. Why?

ROD: Well, I thought we could cook another of our famous suppers and invite Barbara and Sue.

PAUL: Oh, no! Not potato salad again! Sorry, Rod, but I really have to read this book.

7 Paul Blake, who is also an Old Cliftonian, received this letter from his old headmaster.

Imagine you are Paul Blake.

1. Write a letter refusing the invitation to the reunion, giving an excuse.
Start like this:

Dear Mr Fowler,
Thank you very much for your invitation to ... on ... I would love to come, but I'm afraid I ...

2. Write another paragraph at the end of the letter, saying what you are doing now (your studies, where you are living, what you would like to do in the future).

CLIFTON COMPREHENSIVE SCHOOL
Clifton, Bristol

Dear Old Cliftonian,
As you may know, we are having a reunion for Old Cliftonians on May 26th from 2 p.m. - 6 p.m. We would be delighted if as many old pupils as possible could attend. Could you please let me know if you can or cannot attend as soon as possible.
I would also be grateful if you could send in a few lines saying what you are doing at the present moment. All news of Old Cliftonians will be printed in the annual school magazine, in June this year.
With many thanks in advance
Yours sincerely
John Fowler
John Fowler
Headmaster

8

LOOKING FOR A BIGGER MARKET

Simon Lister reports on a new project in Europe.

Western Aeronautics, a company which is based in Bristol, is planning to enter the European market in a big way. At the moment, Western, who produce small electrical components, are making all the cabin lighting equipment for the British Aircraft Corporation in a deal which involves several million pounds. The contract with BAC means that there are now better employment prospects in an area which was badly hit by the recession.

As a part of the future development of the company, the Western board of directors are in the process of setting up a second factory in Toulouse, France. As Peter Chester (photo left), Managing Director at Western, says, 'With a small firm such as ours, we shouldn't put all our eggs in one basket. We need to expand the area of our operations.'

Peter Chester, together with Freda Curtis, Personnel Director, and a team of experts, is now based in Toulouse for a six month period to examine the needs of the French aircraft industry.

Freda Curtis explains, 'We want to avoid problems later on, so we are making a very detailed investigation. The French authorities are being very helpful. Back in Bristol, we are now looking for skilled people to go to work in Toulouse. I don't think we are going to have any problems finding staff. Most people enjoy a challenge, especially when it involves making a living in another country.'

1. Use the article to make a list of the questions the reporter asked to get these answers from Peter Chester:

1. I'm the Managing Director at Western.
2. In Bristol.
3. We're setting up a second factory in Toulouse.
   How is Western planning to ...?
4. I'm studying the needs of the French aircraft industry, mainly.
5. Oh yes, very helpful indeed ...
6. That's right, skilled craftsmen and production people.

2. Find words in the text that match these dictionary definitions:

1. a period of reduced activity of trade
2. an arrangement to the advantage of both sides, often in business
3. to make all one's plans depend on the success of one thing
4. chances, expectations

9 Game: Categories

	B	S	T
Country:	Belgium		
City:	Bristol		
Name:	Barbara		
Singer or group:	Bananarama		
Name of car:	Buick		
Food:	Bread		
Sport or sport's personality:	Badminton		

You have 5 minutes!
Find names or words beginning with S and T to fit each category.

Unit 12 Home again!

🔲 **Dialogue**

ROD: Hello, Barbara! Welcome back! You look
marvellous.

BARBARA: Rod! What a surprise! It's lovely to see you
again.

ROD: Sorry I didn't telephone you before you left,
but I didn't have time, in fact ...

BARBARA: Oh, that's all right. Forget it!

ROD: Well, how was Italy?

BARBARA: Fun, but tiring. Milan was interesting.
It's bigger than I expected. Noisier and
dirtier, too.

ROD: And Florence? What did you think of
Florence?

BARBARA: Well, I've never been there before.
I thought it was beautiful. More beautiful
than Paris, in fact. Have you ever been
to Italy?

ROD: No, never. I'd really like to go to Rome.
Well, the car's in the car park. Is this all
your luggage?

BARBARA: Yes, but the suitcase is very heavy.

ROD: Barbara! What's in it? Stones?

BARBARA: No, just twenty pairs of shoes! Oh, it *is*
nice to see you again, Rod!

Set 1 Apologies

> **1.** Sorry I didn't telephone you, but I didn't have time.
> Oh, that's all right. Forget it!

Apologise for	Explanations
a) not doing your homework	You forgot. didn't have time. lost your book.
b) missing the train	You didn't wake up in time. couldn't get a taxi. Your watch was slow. timetable was out of date.
c) not writing while you were away	You forgot. were very busy. lost the address.
d) not meeting your friend as you had arranged	You overslept. got the time of arrival wrong. had to help your parents.

Work in pairs. Make apologies to your partner, choosing different explanations. Your partner accepts your apology like this:
Sorry I didn't do my homework, but I forgot.
Oh, that's all right.

2. Roleplay these situations in pairs.
a) Apologise and explain to a friend why you didn't come to classes last week.
b) Apologise and explain to a friend why you didn't write or telephone him/her while you were away in London.
c) Apologise and explain to your employer why you arrived half an hour late for work this morning.

Answer:
1. Where did Rod meet Barbara?
2. Why didn't Rod telephone Barbara before she left?
3. What did he say when he apologised?
4. What did Barbara think of Italy?
5. What did she think of Milan?
6. Has Rod ever been to Italy?
7. Where's Rod's car?
8. Why is Barbara's suitcase heavy?
9. Is Barbara pleased to see Rod?

Set 2 Comparisons

> **1.** Milan is bigger than I expected. Noisier and
> dirtier, too.
> I think Florence is more beautiful than Paris.

FACTS ABOUT PLACES, PEOPLE AND THINGS

size		depth		width	
big	bigger	deep	deeper	narrow	narrower
large	larger			wide	wider
small	smaller				
thin	thinner				

temperature		height		length	
hot	hotter	tall	taller	long	longer
warm	warmer	high	higher	wide	wider
mild	milder	short	shorter		
cool	cooler				
cold	colder				

OPINIONS ABOUT PLACES, PEOPLE AND THINGS

dirty	dirtier	good	better	fast	faster
clean	cleaner	bad	worse	slow	slower
noisy	noisier	lively	livelier	fat	fatter
ugly	uglier	dull	duller		
		cheap	cheaper		

beautiful	more/less beautiful
interesting	more/less interesting
depressing	more/less depressing
expensive	more/less expensive
exciting	more/less exciting

Compare the features of countries like this:
China/large/Japan   China is larger than Japan.

1. England/small/France
2. London/big/Rome
3. Skyscrapers in New York/tall/buildings in London
4. The River Avon/short/the Thames
5. The Mississippi/long/the Nile
6. Mount Everest/high/Mont Blanc
7. The South of France/hot/the North
8. The Mediterranean/warm/the North Sea
9. The air at night/cool/the sea at night
10. Winters in Scandinavia/cold/the winters in Europe
11. English winters/mild/Scottish winters
12. The Aegean/warm/the Baltic

**2. Compare your country with any other country
you know well. Compare these features:**

population	roads	geographical features
climate	people	(mountains, rivers, lakes)
cities and towns	food	*anything else*
the standard of living		

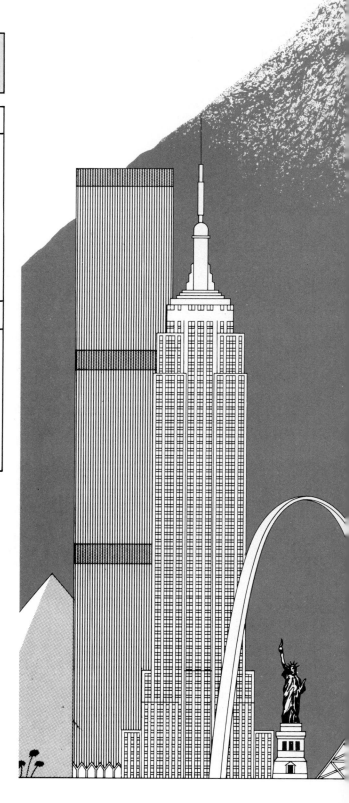

3. In pairs, read your comparisons to your partner. Your partner agrees, disagrees or responds like this:

Spain is larger than Portugal, isn't it?
Yes, that's true.
And the people in Portugal are livelier than
the people in Spain.
Yes, I agree. *or* No, I don't agree. I think the people in
Spain are livelier.
However, the food in Spain is less expensive than the
food in Portugal.
Really? That's interesting. I didn't know that.

4. What comparisons would you make to a friend who can't decide between:

1.	taking a boating holiday down the Rhine in Germany	AND	taking a walking holiday in the English Lake District?

(useful adjectives: *beautiful, warm, cold, cheap, relaxing*)

2.	travelling by train through Europe	AND	travelling by car through Europe?

(cheap, fast, comfortable, relaxing)

3.	wanting a career as a doctor	AND	wanting a career as a social worker?

(interesting, well-paid, rewarding)

4.	joining a dance exercise (aerobics) class	AND	taking up jogging?

(energetic, sociable, difficult, fun, expensive, snobbish)

Make comparisons like this:
It's warmer in Germany than in the Lake District. And
it's more beautiful too.
On the other hand, camping is less relaxing.

5. Test your knowledge!
1. Which is bigger, Concorde or a Boeing 747?
2. Which is older, the Pyramids or Stonehenge?
3. Which is taller, the Empire State Building or the World Trade Centre?
4. Which is more fattening, a quarter of a glass of whisky or a whole glass of milk?
5. Which is nearer the earth, Venus or Mars?
6. Which is less fattening, a glass of wine or a glass of beer?
7. Which runs faster, a cheetah or an antelope?
8 Which is larger, the Taj Mahal or St Peter's in the Vatican?

Set 3 Experiences and impressions

A: Have you ever been to Britain?
B: Yes, I have. I went there last summer, actually.
A: Did you enjoy it?
B: I thought it was wonderful!
A: Do you travel a lot?

A: Have you ever eaten snails?
B: No, never. Have you?
A: Yes, once, when I went to a French restaurant.
B: What did you think of them?
A: Actually, I didn't like them very much. There was too much garlic.

Work in pairs. Ask and talk about these things:

TRAVEL

Have you ever been to ...?
When did you go?
Was it the first time, or have you been there before?
Did you enjoy it?
Do you travel a lot?

Examples
France
The Far East
Britain
Europe
..........?

FOOD AND DRINK

Have you ever { tried ...?
eaten ...?
drunk ...?

Did you like it?
What did you think of it?
Do you eat a lot of unusual food?

Indian food
Chinese food
snails
Guinness
seaweed
raw fish
..........?

ACTIVITIES AND SPORT

Have you ever done any ...?
Do/did you enjoy it?
How did you get on?
Do you do a lot of ...?

sailing
water skiing
horse riding
fishing
wind surfing
camping
carpentry
dressmaking
mountain climbing
skate boarding
jazz dancing
..........?

THE SUPERNATURAL

Have you ever seen { a ghost?
a poltergeist?

experienced something you can't explain?

said to yourself 'This has happened before'?

What happened?
Do you believe in the supernatural?

Reading

Mona Laird, a friend of Barbara's, is a writer. She sometimes writes romantic short stories. Here is an extract from one story.

Clarissa

continuing our romantic serial
For new readers: Clarissa Hopper is on her way back to England after a visit to Italy. Now read on.

Clarissa looked out of the taxi window at the wet road. It was still raining. She was looking forward to getting home after a busy and tiring week in Italy.

The taxi began to slow down. Then the handsome brown-eyed driver turned round to face Clarissa and said, 'Terminal, signorina.' He smiled. The taxi stopped outside the terminal and Clarissa got out. While she was finding some money in her purse, the driver took out her luggage. 'That's the last of my lira,' thought Clarissa sadly as she paid her fare.

She picked up her suitcase, passed through the automatic doors and entered the terminal building. She felt as if she had just crossed the border of Italy. The British Airways check-in desk was near the entrance. After checking-in her luggage, she went to buy some magazines. Then she went through passport control and the security check and into the departure lounge.

She saw from the television screens that her flight was not yet boarding. There was still half an hour before her flight left. While she was waiting she bought some duty-free goods for her parents — some wine, some olives and some salami for herself. She thought suddenly of Simon. 'Perhaps I ought to buy something for Simon. But he never telephoned me before I left, so . . .'

'British Airways announce the departure of Flight BA677 to London Heathrow. Will all passengers please proceed to Gate 11. Flight BA677 to London Heathrow is now boarding.'

It was time to leave. After waiting in the queue with the other passengers, Clarissa got her seat number in the non-smoking section and walked down the corridor and onto the plane. Her seat was next to the window and the emergency exit. With relief she sat down and fastened her safety belt. But she still felt nervous. She travelled by plane so often, but she still hated every moment of it. She couldn't understand why she was afraid of flying.

While the plane was taking off, she closed her eyes, but when the plane was in the air she began to relax. She pressed the button at the side of her seat, lay back and opened her eyes again. 'I wonder if Simon's going to come and meet me at the airport. It's so much nicer to come home when you know there's someone to meet you and help you with your luggage. All those books! They're heavier than I expected. Anyway, I don't really care if he's there or not. . . Oh, well, back to business!' Clarissa took out her calculator.

Ping! The sound of a bell woke Clarissa from her dreams. 'Ladies and Gentlemen, we are now approaching London Heathrow. Will you please fasten your seatbelts and extinguish all cigarettes. Kindly refrain from smoking until you are inside the terminal building.'

When the plane landed and came to a standtill Clarissa saw that outside the sun was shining and the sky was clear. It was going to be a perfect day.

Unit 12

1. Before buying some magazines, she checked in her luggage.

=

After checking in her luggage, she went to buy some magazines.

Link these pairs of sentences in two ways. First use Before ...ing. **Then use** After ...ing.
1. First she bought some magazines. Then she went through passport control.
2. First she bought some duty-free goods. Then she went to the departure lounge.
3. First she collected her seat number. Then she boarded the plane.

2. While she was waiting for her flight to be called, she bought some duty-free goods.

Link these pairs of sentences with While ... was ...ing.
1. Clarissa looked for some money. The driver got out her luggage.
2. She waited in the departure lounge. She had a cup of coffee.
3. The plane took off. Clarissa closed her eyes.

3. When the plane landed, she saw the sun was shining.

Link these pairs of sentences with When.
1. She found that her seat was near the emergency exit. She sat down with relief.
2. The plane took off. She felt nervous.
3. The plane was in the air. She began to relax.

4. Write an account of Clarissa's arrival at London airport. Link these events with when, while, before, after **and** then.

Clarissa:
waited for most of the passengers to get off
unfastened her seat belt
picked up her hand luggage
left the plane
went through passport control
waited for her luggage
(at the same time) phoned her parents
found a luggage trolley
collected her luggage
went through Customs
saw Simon waiting at the arrival gate

Roleplay

In pairs, make a list of five films you have seen recently or heard about. Talk about two of the films like this:

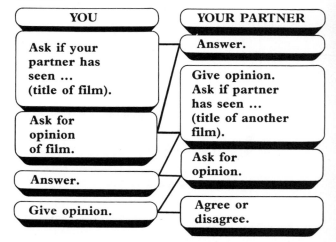

YOU	YOUR PARTNER
Ask if your partner has seen ... (title of film).	Answer.
	Give opinion. Ask if partner has seen ... (title of another film).
Ask for opinion of film.	
	Ask for opinion.
Answer.	
Give opinion.	Agree or disagree.

Listening

John is British, but he has worked in Japan. Etsuko is Japanese from Osaka, but she is studying in Britain. Listen to them comparing life as they see it in the two countries. Make notes about the features of each country they mention and the comparisons they make.

	THE FEATURES	COMPARISONS
John:	The people in Japan are	
Etsuko:	The summer in England is	

Write paragraphs using your notes, like this:
John says that, in his experience, the ...
Etsuko says that, in her experience, the ...

Writing

Think of a journey you have made recently.
First make notes of the things you did and the things that happened. Organise your composition like this:

PARAGRAPH 1: Say when your journey took place, where you went, with whom and how.
PARAGRAPH 2: Describe the journey and any special incidents that occurred. Use linking words like: before, after, while and when.
PARAGRAPH 3: Say what you thought of the journey and any conclusions you came to. Also give any advice you think necessary to people going on the same journey.

Oral exercises

1. Apologise and give an explanation
You didn't have time to send your friend a postcard.
Sorry I didn't send you a postcard, but I didn't have time.
That's OK.
You forgot to telephone your friend.
Sorry I didn't telephone, but I forgot.
That's all right.

1. You didn't have time to send your friend a postcard.
2. You forgot to telephone your friend.
3. You overslept so you missed the bus. Apologise to your boss.
4. Your watch was slow and you were late for work. Apologise to your boss.
5. You were ill last week, so you didn't come to classes. Apologise to your teacher.
6. You didn't know the time of the train, so you didn't meet your sister at the station.

2. Make comparisons about the weather
Talk about the weather.
What was the weather like in Cairo? Hot, I suppose?
Yes, it was much hotter than we expected.
So you went to the south of France for Christmas?
Well, they say it's quite mild there.
Yes, it was much milder than we expected.

1. Cairo/hot
2. South of France at Christmas/mild
3. Soviet Union in winter/cold
4. Ireland/wet
5. Mexico in winter/cool
6. England/warm

3. Compare experiences
You have just come back from your holiday in Spain.
You always go there every year.

What was the weather like? Good?
Yes, much better than last year.
And what about the shops? Were they expensive?
Yes, much more expensive than last year.

1. weather/good
2. shops/expensive
3. sea/nice and clean
4. beaches/crowded
5. people at the hotel/interesting
6. food/bad

Extra work
Re-express 2, 4 and 5, like this:
2. What about the shops? Were they expensive?
   Well, they were less expensive than I expected.

4. Give a contrasting comparison
You have been on holiday with friends.
Match the pairs of opposite adjectives to make your comparisons.

good	cheap	exciting	beautiful
interesting	dirty	dull	ugly
expensive	clean	bad	depressing

The food was better than I expected.
Well, I thought it was rather bad.
Did you? Well, the discos were exciting.
Well, I thought they were rather depressing.

1. The food was better than I expected.
2. The discos were exciting.
3. Mind you, the drinks were expensive.
4. And the beaches were a bit dirty.
5. Still, I thought the countryside was interesting.
6. At least the modern hotels were really beautiful.

5. Ask about people's experience
Ask about pictures 1—6.
1. *Have you ever done any horse riding?*
   Yes, I have. Once.
   How did you get on?
   Quite well, in fact.

2. *Have you ever done any sailing?*
   Yes, I do a lot of sailing.
   Oh, do you enjoy it?
   Yes, very much.

Unit 13 Mandy is missing_____

🔲 **Dialogue Part 1**

At Clifton Police Station. The telephone rings...

POLICEMAN: Clifton Police Station. Can I help you?

MRS INGRAMS: Yes. It's about my daughter, Mandy. She went to school this morning and she hasn't arrived yet, and it's eleven o'clock and...

POLICEMAN: Just a moment, Mrs...?

MRS INGRAMS: Mrs Ingrams. Joan Ingrams, 57 Bath Road.

POLICEMAN: Thank you. Now Mrs Ingrams, what exactly is the matter?

MRS INGRAMS: Well, Mandy — that's my little daughter — left home this morning at about a quarter to nine. Then her teacher telephoned me about a quarter of an hour ago and asked if Mandy was ill. I said, 'No. Why?' And then she said, 'Well, Mandy hasn't come to school yet.' So I said I didn't know where she was. Then I decided to ring you.

POLICEMAN: Quite right. Perhaps she went home to a friend? Have you asked your neighbours?

MRS INGRAMS: Yes, I have. I've rung all the neighbours and they haven't seen her, and their children are all at school and...

POLICEMAN: I see. Now, let's have a few details. How old is Mandy?

MRS INGRAMS: She's six.

POLICEMAN: And what does she look like?

MRS INGRAMS: She's got fair hair, long fair hair with a ribbon in it — a red ribbon — er... she's got blue eyes...

POLICEMAN: And what's she wearing?

MRS INGRAMS: She's wearing a grey coat and brown shoes, red tights — er . . . green skirt and a red sweater. Yes, that's right.

POLICEMAN: We'll do our best to find her, Mrs Ingrams. I expect she's just playing truant. Now you keep calm and we'll telephone you as soon as we find her.

MRS INGRAMS: Thank you. Goodbye.

POLICEMAN: Goodbye, Mrs Ingrams. And try not to worry.

1. Answer:
1. Who is Mandy?
2. Why is Mrs Ingrams ringing the police station?
3. When did she leave home that morning?
4. Where was she going?
5. What time did Mandy's teacher phone?
6. Why did she phone?
7. Who has Mrs Ingrams asked about Mandy?
8. What did they say?

2. Use the dialogue to complete the police form.

CLIFTON POLICE STATION	MISSING PERSONS
Name:	Sex:
Age:	Next of kin:
Type of clothing — colour	
1.	
2.	
3.	
4.	
5.	
Other details	

Set 1 Narration: past events

POLICE REPORT FROM WITNESS

Missing person
Mandy Ingrams

Date: 25/9

Name of witness: *Mrs Joan Ingrams*
51 Bath Road, Bristol

Relationship: *Mother of missing child*

Mrs I. – got up at 7.30. Had breakfast with family – husband and son, Mark, 4 years old. Daughter Mandy got ready for school, put on grey coat, said it was teacher's birthday, wanted to buy some flowers. Mrs I. gave her 20p. M. left house at 8.45. School is 5 minutes walk from house. Mrs I. has not seen her since then.

POLICE REPORT FROM WITNESS

Missing person
Mandy Ingrams

Date: 25/9

Name of witness: *Mrs Marjorie Hawkins, The Sweet Shop, Central Parade, London Road, Bristol.*

Relationship: *None.*

Mrs. H. – owns sweet shop, Central Parade. Opened shop at 9. Little girl wearing grey coat came in. Red ribbon in hair. Girl had 20p. Girl asked, 'Do you sell flowers?' Mrs H. said 'No, I don't, but there are some pretty wild flowers near the canal.' Girl said, 'Thank you.'
Left shop at 9.10

Roleplay 1

Work in pairs. You are the policeman, your partner is Mrs Ingrams. Use the notes in the Police Report to interview Mrs Ingrams. Ask questions like:

What time did you get up?
What did you do then?
Did your husband take Mandy to school?
What did Mandy do then?
Did she say anything before she left?
Did you give her any money?
When did Mandy leave the house?
How far away is the school?
Have you seen her since?

Roleplay 2

Work in pairs. You are the policeman, your partner is Mrs Hawkins. Use the notes in the Police Report to interview Mrs Hawkins. Ask questions like:

What do you do?
What time did you open your shop this morning?
Did a little girl come into the shop?
What was she wearing?
How much money did she have?
What did she say?
What did you say?
Did she buy anything?
What time did she leave the shop?

POLICE REPORT FROM WITNESS

Missing person
Mandy Ingrams

Date: 25/9

Name of witness: Jack Priestman
5 Canal Lane, Bristol.

Relationship: None

Mr. P. — ....

Listening

Listen to the policeman interviewing another witness, Jack Priestman. Make notes like those in the Police Reports for the other witnesses, Mrs Ingrams and Mrs Hawkins.

Reading

After interviewing the three witnesses, the policeman types out his notes in full. Read the report of his interview with Mrs Ingrams.

Mrs Joan Ingrams who lives at 57, Bath Road, Bristol, is the mother of the missing child. On the morning of September 25th she got up at 7.30. Then she had breakfast with her family – her husband and her son, Mark. Then her daughter, Mandy, got ready for school. She put on her grey coat. Mandy said that it was her teacher's birthday. Mrs Ingrams gave Mandy 20p and Mandy left the house at 8.45. Mandy's school is about five minutes' walk from the house. Mrs Ingrams did not see her daughter again.

Writing

Write reports for one of the other two interviews.

Dialogue Part 2

POLICEMAN: Have you found anything?
POLICEWOMAN: No, nothing. Have you checked with the station?
POLICEMAN: They haven't found anything either. Nobody has seen her. I think...
POLICEWOMAN: Wait a minute! Stop the engine. Look! Flowers! There are some flowers on the bank of the canal.
POLICEMAN: The woman in the sweetshop said something about flowers. You don't think...
POLICEWOMAN: Mandy saw some flowers and climbed down to pick them. Then she slipped and...
POLICEMAN: ...fell in! It's possible. Poor little thing! Ah, here's the other launch. Any luck?
PATROLMAN: I don't know. We've just found this. It was floating in the water.
POLICEWOMAN: What is it?
PATROLMAN: Ribbon. It's a piece of red ribbon...
POLICEWOMAN: Oh, no!
POLICEMAN: You don't think she's...
POLICEWOMAN: Quick! Contact the police station. Tell them we need two divers and tell them it's urgent!

Answer:
1. Why are the flowers important?
2. Why is the red ribbon important?
3. Why do the police need two divers?
4. How do they think the accident happened?

95

Set 2 Description: appearance

> **1.** What does she look like? She's got fair hair.
> What's she wearing? She's wearing a raincoat.

In pairs, talk about the people in the pictures.
A: Has she/he got long hair?
B: Yes, that's right. Long brown hair.
A: Is she/he wearing shoes?
B: No. Boots. Green boots.

2. Make notes to describe your partner using the following headings:
Colour of hair   Hair style   Colour of eyes
Colour of clothing   Type of clothing

Roleplay
You arrive at London Airport. You are expecting a friend, Susan, to meet you at the arrival gate. She isn't there, so you wait half an hour and then telephone her. Susan's brother answers the telephone.

YOU	SUSAN'S BROTHER
Ask to speak to Susan.	
	Say Susan is out and ask who is speaking.
Say who you are and explain the problem.	
	Say Susan had to go to work. Offer to meet at airport. Ask what person looks like. Ask what person is wearing.
Describe your appearance.	
	Say what you look like and what you are wearing. Arrange to meet at the Information Desk.

Types of clothes

coat	trainers
cardigan	jeans
pullover	belt
tracksuit	boots
skirt	jacket
tights	socks
raincoat	high/low
dress	heeled shoes
trousers	

Style of clothes

short-sleeved
long-sleeved
sleeveless

Set 3 Completed actions

1.	Have you been to the cinema recently?	No, I haven't.
	Have you watched TV recently?	Yes, I have.
	What programmes did you watch?	A football match/ a nature programme/ a quiz game and a film about drug smuggling.

How do you spend your free time?
Think about the past few days.

Have you ... recently?	Yes	No	(if yes)
1. been to the cinema or theatre			What did you see? When?
2. watched TV			What did you watch?
3. read a book or part of a book			What was it about?
4. bought any books or records			What did you buy? Where?
5. bought any clothes			What did you buy? What are the clothes like?
6. been to a lecture or meeting			What was it about?
7. done any sporting activitites			What did you do? Were you in a team?
8. invited any friends home			Who did you invite? What sort of occasion was it?
9. written a letter			Who did you write to?
10. done anything else interesting			What did you do?

Work in pairs. Ask your partner about his/her recent activities using the chart. Make notes of the answers. Ask like this:
Have you seen any good films recently?
Yes, I have.
What did you see?
I saw *ET* at the cinema, and *Gone With the Wind* on TV.

Hair styles

wavy	a ponytail
curly	in bunches
straight	in plaits
fringe	

2. Tell the rest of the class what your partner has done, like this:
Peter has done quite a lot of things in his spare time recently. He has been to the cinema to see *Supergirl* and played a game of volleyball. He has visited his cousins and has eaten out in a pizzeria. He has also read a few chapters of a book about diamond smuggling.

Writing
Write two paragraphs:
1. about the things your partner has done recently.
2. about the things you have done recently.

Listening
Listen to these people talking about their recent activities and list what they have done.

Reading

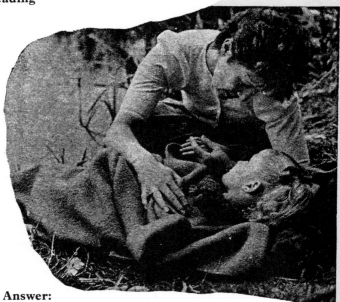

BRISTOL GIRL IN CANAL DRAMA

by Mike Sanders

MANDY INGRAMS, a pretty, fair-haired, six-year-old girl, nearly drowned last Wednesday in the canal in Moss Park. Mandy was on her way to school. It was her teacher's birthday and Mandy wanted to buy her some flowers. She went to the local sweet shop on Central Estate, but the owner, Mrs Marjorie Hawkins, told her that she did not sell flowers. So Mandy went to the bank of the canal in Moss Park to pick some wild flowers for her teacher.

UNCONSCIOUS
Three hours later, the police found Mandy. She was lying near the water and she was unconscious. She also had a broken leg. She was lying three inches from the edge of the canal. Police Constable Peggy Booth told me, 'Mandy is very lucky to be alive. She had a very narrow escape.'
Mandy is now in the children's ward at Bristol General Hospital.

NEXT TIME?
Once again, the Moss Park Canal is the scene of a near fatal accident. The canal passes very close to Saint John's First School. At this point it is over two metres deep. There are no fences. In fact, there is nothing to stop small children from falling into the water. It is time for the local authorities to do something about this dangerous playground. The next little Mandy may not be so lucky.

1. Answer:
1. How does the reporter describe Mandy?
2. Did she drown?
3. Where did the police find her?
4. Was she hurt?
5. Why is the canal dangerous?

2. Make questions for these answers.
1. The owner of the sweetshop.
2. Because she wanted to pick some flowers for her teacher.
3. At the edge of the canal.
4. In the children's ward at Bristol General Hospital.
5. About two metres.

3. Group work
Is there a dangerous playground where you live? If so, how can it be made less dangerous?
Who do you think was responsible for what happened to Mandy?

Writing
Write the story of Mandy's accident from the time she left home in the morning until the time the police found her. Use:
a) the dialogues and the pictures
b) the Police Reports from the witnesses
c) the newspaper article

Link events with when and while, like this:

When Mandy did not arrive at school, her teacher telephoned Mrs Ingrams.
While the police were searching, Mandy was lying unconscious near the edge of the canal.

Oral exercises

1. Ask people about their taste in clothes
Barbara, do you like wearing dresses or jeans?
Oh, I like wearing jeans.
And do you like wearing tee-shirts or blouses?
Well, it depends.

Ask Barbara about:
1. dresses   jeans
2. tee-shirts   blouses
3. sweaters   cardigans

Ask Rod about:
1. trousers   jeans
2. short-sleeved shirts   long-sleeved shirts
3. boots   shoes

2. Give your opinion about clothes and appearance (Open exercise)
Do you like long or short hair?
(Long hair — definitely.)
Do you like wearing tee-shirts?
(No, I don't, not at all.)

1. Do you like long or short hair?
2. Do you like wearing tee-shirts?
3. Do you like wearing jeans?
4. Do you like boots, sandals, or shoes?
5. What sort of hairstyle do you like?
6. What sort of clothes do you wear most of the time?

3. Apologise for not completing certain activities
The sergeant at Clifton Police Station is talking to one of the policemen.

Have you looked on the bank?
Not yet, I'm afraid. I'm just going to look there.
And have you talked to the woman in the sweetshop?
Not yet, I'm afraid. I'm just going to talk to her.

1. look on the bank
2. talk to the woman in the sweetshop
3. go to the school
4. speak to Jack Priestman
5. ring Mandy's father
6. tell Mrs Ingrams what's happening

4. Say that you have completed certain activities
Two policemen are searching for Mandy.

What about looking on the bank?
I've just looked there.
How about talking to the woman in the sweetshop?
I've just talked to her.

1. look on the bank
2. talk to the woman in the sweetshop
3. go to the school
4. speak to Jack Priestman
5. ring Mandy's father
6. tell Mrs Ingrams what's happening

5. Check details
You are with Barbara just before she leaves her flat to go to Italy. Check that she has done things.

Have you closed all the windows, Barbara?
Yes, I have. I've just done it.
Have you unplugged the TV?
Yes.

Check that Barbara has done these things on your list:
1. close all windows   4. turn off lights
2. unplug TV   5. lock back door
3. turn off fridge   6. cancel newspapers

Open dialogue
Talk to Barbara.
BARBARA: Hi! How are you?
YOU: ....
BARBARA: What sort of week have you had?
YOU: ....
BARBARA: I've just come back from Italy.
YOU: ....
BARBARA: Have you been anywhere exciting this year?
YOU: ....
BARBARA: What about your next holidays? Where are you going?
YOU: ....
BARBARA: Have you ever been there before?
YOU: ....
BARBARA: Actually, I went to Italy on business—to buy some shoes.
         Are you interested in shoes?
YOU: ....
BARBARA: Have you bought anything recently?
YOU: ....
BARBARA: Oh, well, why don't you come and see my boutique sometime?
         See if you like my Italian shoes. Bye!

Unit 14 Star

🔊 Dialogue

Mike Sanders interviews Laura Dennison, a folk singer, after a concert.

MIKE: That was a beautiful performance, Laura. And welcome back to Bristol.

LAURA: Thank you. Now, your questions. Oh, good, you've got my press release.

MIKE: Yes. You were born here in Bristol, weren't you, in 1955?

LAURA: That's right. I was born not far from this theatre, actually. But I grew up in the suburbs.

MIKE: And your parents?

LAURA: They came from Ireland originally. My father was a Customs Officer at the docks.

MIKE: Is he still there?

LAURA: No, he died about three years ago.

MIKE: Have you got any brothers or sisters?

LAURA: No, I'm an only child.

MIKE: Mm. And then you went to university?

LAURA: Yes, for three years. That's where I wrote the song 'The Price of Peace'.

MIKE: And got married!

LAURA: Yes.

MIKE: How long have you been singing professionally?

LAURA: Oh, quite a long time! Actually I've been singing professionally since 1978 when I recorded my first song.

MIKE: And now you're a world famous star, a composer and a mother. How do you manage to do it?

LAURA: Do what?

MIKE: Combine a career with a family?

LAURA: Are you married with a family, Mr Sanders?

MIKE: Yes, but...

LAURA: Well, do you find it difficult to be a journalist *and* a father?

MIKE: But...

LAURA: Think about it, Mr Sanders. Goodbye!

Answer:

1. Did Laura grow up in the country?
2. What nationality were her parents?
3. What did her father do?
4. Is he still alive?
5. Does Laura come from a big family?
6. Where did she compose her first song?
7. Where did Laura meet her husband?

PAX RECORDS
Press Release

LAURA DENNISON

1955 Born in Bristol
1960 Started school
1973 Went to Bristol University
1974 Joined a folk group
1975 Married Tony Harper
1976 Left university
1977 Won folk song competition
1978 Birth of daughter, Jody
　　 Recorded song 'The Price of Peace'
　　 (Number 3 in Top Twenty)
1979 American, South American and European
　　 tours
1983 Went to live in Los Angeles

Laura's new single 'Women are people too' is in your record shop NOW

Set 1 Past events

> **1.** She was born *in* 1955.
> Her father died three years *ago*.
> She went to university *for* three years.
> She has been singing professionally *since* 1978.

In pairs, ask and answer questions about Laura Dennison's life, using the press release.
a) Use in with dates, like this:
When did Laura go to university?
In 1973.
When did she get married?
When did she win the folk song competition?
When did she tour South America?
When did she go to live in America?

b) Use ago with the numbers of years. Count back, like this:
When did Laura join the folk group?
(If it is 1984 now) Ten years ago.
When did she leave university?
When did she record her first song?
When did she tour America?

c) Use for with numbers of years. Count up, like this:
How long did Laura go to school for?
For 13 years.
How long did she go to university for?
How long has she been married for?

d) Use since with dates, like this:
How long has Laura been singing?
She has been singing since 1974.
How long has she been singing professionally?
How long has she been living in America?

2. In pairs, ask and answer these questions about your past life.

When did you first start school? *When I was ...* or *In ...*
When did you leave school? *... ago.* or *I haven't left yet.*
How long did you stay at school? or How long have you been at school? *For ... years.*
How long have you been living in your present home. *I have been living there for/since ...*
How long have you been studying at this school? *For/since ...*
How long have you been learning English in this class? *For/since ...*
How long have you been learning English with your present teacher? *For/since ...*
How long have you been using this book? *For/since ...*

Set 2 Biographies

RECORD NEWS

12th November, 1968 New Musical Express—Page 5

LAURA DENNISON, famous singer and star of the Top Twenty, was born in Bristol. Her parents originally came from Ireland. Laura's father was a Customs Officer in the Bristol docks. Unfortunately, he died a few years ago.

Laura, who is an only child, grew up in the suburbs of Bristol. She started her education at a local school and then moved to a large, modern comprehensive school in another part of the city.

After leaving school when she was 18, Laura went to Bristol University for three years to study history and economics. While she was at university, Laura joined a university folk group and started singing. It was at this time that she wrote her famous song 'The Price of Peace'. Soon after finishing her university career, Laura joined another group and began to earn money with her performances and with her songs.

When she was 21, Laura was married to Tony Harper who was also a student. Laura and Tony have two children — a daughter, Jody, and a son, Daniel. For several years the Harper family have been living in a beautiful farm house in the country outside Bristol, but recently they decided to leave Britain and move to Los Angeles.

1.

Where were you born?	I was born in Bristol.
Where did you grow up?	I grew up in Bristol.
Where did you go to school?	I went to a comprehensive school.
What did you do after that?	I got a job.
	I went to business college.
	I started an apprenticeship.

Complete this chart for yourself:

Background:	I was born in ... *(place, country)*
Early life:	I grew up in ... I went to school at ... for ...
Career:	After studying at ... *(school)*, I left and went to ... *(place of work, college, university)* to work/study.
Other information:	I am an only child/I have got ... *(brothers/sisters, etc.)*

2. There are four paragraphs in Mike Sanders' article. Which paragraph is about:

Laura's career?
Laura's background?
Other information about Laura?
Laura's early life?

🔈 **Listening**

Listen to the Radio Bristol quiz 'Alive or Dead?' Try to guess the name of the person *before* the members of the quiz panel. Make notes:

Is the person alive or dead?
real or fictional?
a man or a woman?

What is his/her nationality?
occupation?

Stop your tape and write down the answer if you think you have guessed it.

Notes for future articles on Bristol personalities

GERALDINE BEVAN – detective story writer
Background – born Edinburgh, Scotland 1938. Father novelist, mother teacher. Parents from Wales originally. Only child.

Early education – village school.
Later education – Edinburgh High School for Girls.
Early career – journalist in Edinburgh, later London.
Later career – Wrote first successful detective story at 20. still writing successful books (all bestsellers)
Other information – won the 'Best Detective Story Writer of the Year' award in 1977. Married – husband now dead.

Note – Miss Bevan does not like talking about her private life.

IVOR JONES – boxer
Background – b. Swansea, South Wales, '55. Father miner, m. shop assistant. Parents living. Middle child of 5 brothers.

Early education – Dock Street Junior School, Swansea.
Later education – Aberdale Comprehensive.
Early career – Left school at 15. Worked in docks. Started boxing in youth club at 17.
Later career – Won light-weight championship – Olympic Gold Medal, Montreal, '76. Became professional '78.
Other information – Married, 2 children, wife gymnastics teacher. Going to leave Britain to live in Spain.

N.B. Ivor <u>likes</u> talking about his family.

Roleplay
Work in pairs. You are a newspaper reporter. Your partner is Geraldine Bevan or Ivor Jones. Interview him/her using the biographical details above. The interviewer should work like this:

Introduce yourself and ask permission to ask some questions; ask where person was born; ask about person's parents; ask about early education; ask about later education; ask about early career; ask about later career; ask permission to ask questions about person's private life; thank person.

Writing
Rod Nelson, who is a Canadian engineer, comes from Ottawa. At the moment he is living in Bristol in the south-west of England. He has been living there for several months. He works in a firm called Western Aeronautics. He has been working there for four months.

Write a similar paragraph about a friend or relative. Say:
1. who they are
2. what they do
3. where they live
4. how long they have been living there
5. where they work/study
6. how long they have been working/studying there

Reading

Elvis Presley

born January 8th 1935
died August 16th 1977
— *"the most dangerous thing
to hit civilisation since the
atom bomb."*

Elvis Aaron Presley was born on January 8th 1935, in East Tupelo, Mississippi. His twin brother died at birth. Elvis grew up in a poor but religious home which was typical of the deep south of the United States. His parents, Vernon and Gladys Presley, were kind and loving.

While he was still a child, Elvis won several talent competitions. Later, after he left school, he worked as a cinema usher and a truck driver. This was the job Elvis always said he liked best.

The first person to realise that Elvis was a good singer was Sam Phillips, the owner of a record company called Sun Records. But the man who really guided Elvis's career was Colonel Tom Parker. Colonel Parker became Elvis's manager in 1955 and soon made him into a world famous rock and roll star.

By 1956, Elvis Presley had won six gold discs. These were the first of many which he won during his life. When he was young, Elvis had many critics — particularly from the older generation. They thought that Elvis was 'dangerous for the morals of young people'. Life — and people's attitudes — have changed since 1956. And Elvis Presley helped to change them. Elvis died suddenly in early middle age. Many people say that he died because he took too many drugs and pills.

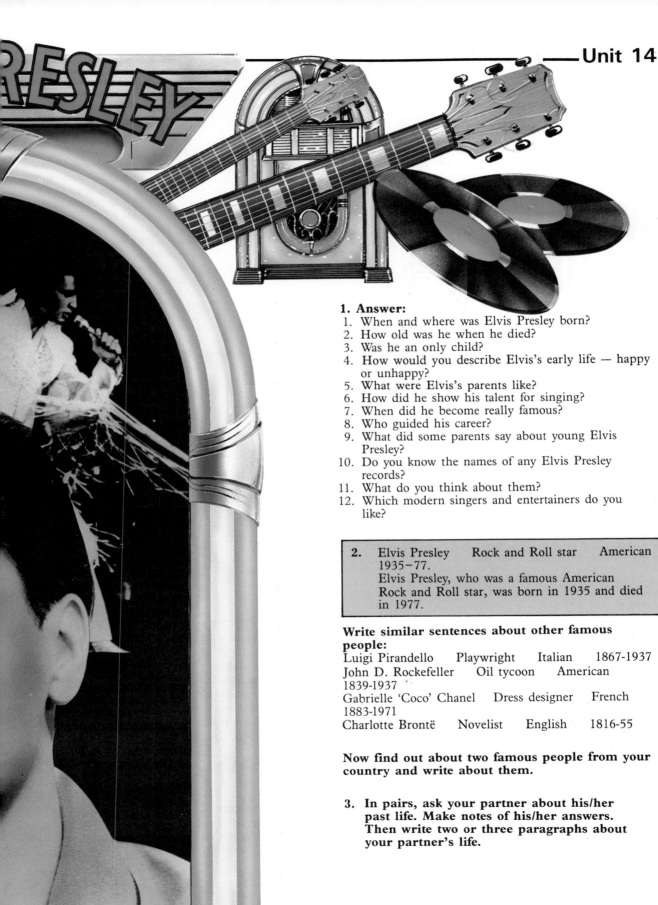

1. Answer:
1. When and where was Elvis Presley born?
2. How old was he when he died?
3. Was he an only child?
4. How would you describe Elvis's early life — happy or unhappy?
5. What were Elvis's parents like?
6. How did he show his talent for singing?
7. When did he become really famous?
8. Who guided his career?
9. What did some parents say about young Elvis Presley?
10. Do you know the names of any Elvis Presley records?
11. What do you think about them?
12. Which modern singers and entertainers do you like?

> **2.** Elvis Presley   Rock and Roll star   American 1935–77.
> Elvis Presley, who was a famous American Rock and Roll star, was born in 1935 and died in 1977.

Write similar sentences about other famous people:
Luigi Pirandello   Playwright   Italian   1867-1937
John D. Rockefeller   Oil tycoon   American 1839-1937
Gabrielle 'Coco' Chanel   Dress designer   French 1883-1971
Charlotte Brontë   Novelist   English   1816-55

Now find out about two famous people from your country and write about them.

3. In pairs, ask your partner about his/her past life. Make notes of his/her answers. Then write two or three paragraphs about your partner's life.

Reading

WINNIE MANDELA

South African (born 1935)

Winnie Mandela is one of the heroines of the black activist movement against the apartheid policies of the South African government. Since her marriage in 1958 to Nelson Mandela, one of South Africa's first black lawyers and a leading member of the African National Congress, the South African police have imprisoned her, stopped her from travelling, kept her in her home, searched and constantly harassed her. Since 1977, they have banished her from her home town of Soweto, and forced her to live in the Orange Free State. She has

no electricity, running water, bath, stove or main drainage.

She has suffered all these things because the police say that she has broken the law. But in reality, they have punished her because she has become, like her husband, a leader of the black nationalist movement. Among other things, she was a founder member of Soweto's Black Parents Association.

Winnie Mandela was brought up in Pondoland, where her father was Minister of Agriculture. She trained as a social worker in Johannesburg. She married Nelson Mandela when he was on trial. The jury acquitted him and the couple enjoyed a brief married life, which included the birth of two daughters. However, the police arrested him again in 1962. Since 1964, Nelson Mandela has been in prison on Robben Island, where Winnie is allowed to visit him only once a month for an hour.

Since 1969, Winnie Mandela has had exactly eight months free of imprisonment or banning orders;* she has used that time to speak out fearlessly and tirelessly, for justice for the black people of South Africa which she believes one day will surely come.

*Rules about where she must live, where she can travel and who she can see.

1. Complete the missing information about Winnie:

Name:	....
Nationality:	....
Date of birth:	....
Training:	....
Father's occupation:	....
Main achievements:	....

Important events and dates:
... Winnie Mandela was born.
1958 ....
... Police arrested Nelson Mandela.
1964 ....
... Police banished her from her home.

2. Answer True or False

1. Winnie Mandela has been a political prisoner for much of her life.
2. She is not allowed to live in her home town.
3. She trained as a lawyer.
4. She lives in a very comfortable house.
5. Her husband was on trial when they married.
6. Winnie comes from a political background.
7. The Mandelas have had a long and happy married life.
8. She is allowed to visit her husband.

Writing
Write a short composition about yourself (an autobiography) or about a person you admire (a biography). Use the notes for the roleplay on page 103 to plan your composition.

Oral exercises

1. Confirm dates

You are Laura Dennison. Mike Sanders is interviewing you. Look at the biographical details in the Press Release. Confirm dates of your past life.

You were born in the middle-fifties, weren't you?
Right. I was born in 1955.
And you went to university in the early seventies?
Right. I went to university in 1973.

1. You were born in the middle fifties, weren't you?
2. And you went to university in the early seventies?
3. You joined a folk group a year after, didn't you?
4. And you got married in the middle seventies?
5. Your daughter was born in the late seventies?
6. And you recorded a hit song in the same year?

2. Talk about general points of time (Open exercise)

When did you start these exercises?
Oh, (just a few minutes) ago.
When did you start this book?
Oh, (a few months) ago.
When was the Second World War?
Oh, (a long time) ago.

1. When did you start these exercises?
2. When did you start this book?
3. When was the Second World War?
4. When was the American Civil War?
5. When was your birthday?
6. When did you start school?

3. Ask how long people have been doing things

I live in Bristol.
Oh, how long have you been living there?
Rod works at Western now.
Oh, how long has he been working there?

1. I live in Bristol.
2. Rod works at Western now.
3. Paul and Sue both study at the polytechnic.
4. We always go to Scotland for our holidays.
5. Barbara works near the new shopping centre.
6. My brother is studying in America.

4. Say when and how long ago you did things

(Open exercise)
When did you first start studying here?
(Four years ago. In 1976.)
And how long have you been in this class?
(For two years. Since 1978.)

1. When did you first start studying here?
2. And how long have you been in this class?
3. When did you begin learning English?
4. And how long have you been using this book?
5. When did you last have a holiday?
6. And how long have you been working in your job?

5. Correct information about people's past lives

Read about Elvis Presley before you do this exercise. Then correct the information.

Elvis was born in 1977.
No, that was when he died.
He died in 1935.
No, that was when he was born.

1. Elvis was born in 1977.
2. He died in 1935.
3. He won several talent competitions when he was a young man.
4. He met Colonel Parker when he was 30.
5. People criticised Elvis when he was middle-aged.

Open dialogue

Talk to Mike Sanders about your past life.
MIKE: Hi! Do you mind if I talk to you?
YOU: ....
MIKE: Well, my questions are quite short. First, I'd like to know where you were born.
YOU: ....
MIKE: I see. And I suppose your parents were born in the same place.
YOU: ....
MIKE: Tell me something about them.
YOU: ....
MIKE: You've got some brothers and sisters, haven't you?
YOU: ....
MIKE: Mm. Where did you first go to school?
YOU: ....
MIKE: Tell me something about your later education.
YOU: ....
MIKE: Do you mind if I ask you some questions about your private life?
YOU: ....
MIKE: Well, actually, I am in a bit of a hurry, so it doesn't matter. I'm afraid I've got to go.

Unit 15 And tomorrow . . .?

BY HAND

Mr and Mrs J. Cooper

Western Aeronautics
Avon Trading Estate, Jubilee Drive, BRISTOL 9.

Tuesday July 15th

Dear Mr and Mrs Cooper,

__Toulouse – travel arrangements__

I enclose details of your travel arrangements for your journey to Toulouse on Saturday 19th July, for you and your wife.

A company car will arrive at your house at 8 a.m. to take you to the airport. The driver will have your tickets. Please make sure that you have your passports.

The plane leaves at 9.30 a.m. and check-in time is at 8.30. Your baggage allowance is 20 kilos each. The flight to Toulouse will take an hour and a half. Breakfast will be served during the flight.

There will be a representative of the company at the arrival gate to meet you at Toulouse. He will have a card saying 'Mr and Mrs J. Cooper – Western Aeronautics'. He will take you to your hotel in the city centre. He will have some French currency for your immediate use.

I hope these arrangements are satisfactory and that you both have a pleasant journey.

Yours sincerely,

Freda Curtis
Freda Curtis
Personnel Officer

Jack Cooper decided to apply for a job in the first European branch of Western Aeronautics in Toulouse in France.

His application was successful and the company made all the travel arrangements for the Coopers to go to France. One morning Jack received a letter with the details of the travel arrangements.

1. Jack and Peggy discussed the journey to France. Complete their conversation, using the information in the letter.

PEGGY: Has the Personnel Officer sent all our travel arrangements for the 19th?
JACK: ....
PEGGY: Then everything is all right, isn't it?
JACK: ....
PEGGY: Well, then, how will we get to the airport?
JACK: ....
PEGGY: But what about the tickets? They haven't sent them — why?
JACK: ....
PEGGY: Oh. I hope he doesn't forget them! Eight o'clock is very early. Will we get anything to eat during the flight?
JACK: ....
PEGGY: Oh, that's good. But what about when we get to the other end — in Toulouse? Will anyone meet us?
JACK: ....
PEGGY: Well, that sounds all right. What about money? We haven't got any French francs yet.
JACK: ....
PEGGY: Fine. And where are we going to stay?
JACK: ....
PEGGY: Lovely! I'm looking forward to that. By the way, Jack, how will the person meeting us know who we are?
JACK: ....
PEGGY: Well, everything is arranged, then. I don't know why you are getting so worried, Jack!

2. Work in pairs. Read the conversation.

🔲 **Listening**
Listen to Jack and Peggy talking about their travel arrangements to France. Look at the conversation in Exercise 1. (Notice that it is different, but the information is the same.)

108

Set 1 Travel

> How will we get to the airport?
> A car will pick us up at 8 a.m.

TRAVEL ARRANGEMENTS

1.	Transport to airport	airport bus taxi company car lift from a friend
2.	Food during flight	breakfast lunch dinner light snack juice/tea/coffee
3.	Arrival and meeting arrangements	travel courier/special bus company representative/ company car/ my parents/ nobody/airport bus
4.	First night accommodation	hotel in city centre my parents' house with friends on the night train to (Milan)

**Work in pairs. Talk about
travel arrangements using the chart.
Ask and answer like this:**

1. How will we get to the airport?
   We'll take the airport bus. *or*
   A friend will give us a lift.

2. Will we get anything to eat during the flight?
   Yes, we'll get ... *or*
   No, we'll only get ...

3. Who will meet us when we arrive?
   A travel courier will meet us with a special bus.

4. Where will we spend the first night?
   We'll spend it at/in/on/with ...

Group work
Find out if anyone in the group is planning to go on a journey in the near future.
If they are, ask them to tell you about their travel arrangements.

🔊 Dialogue

Friday 18th July, at the Coopers' house.

PEGGY: Get the glasses out, Jack. They'll be here soon.

JACK: You know, Peggy, I don't think Rod will come. They've had another row.

PEGGY: Nonsense! It was only a little row! I'm quite sure he'll come to say goodbye to us.

(Doorbell rings. Jack opens the door.)

BARBARA: Hi!

JACK: You're alone, are you!

BARBARA: Yes.

JACK: Where's Rod?

PEGGY: Please, Jack...

BARBARA: Oh, he's getting some wine from the off-licence. He won't be a moment. Just think mum! By this time tomorrow, you'll both be in France!

PEGGY: Yes. Oh dear! I'll miss all my friends.

BARBARA: No, you won't. I'm sure you won't. Well, only for a bit.

JACK: I think we'll be very happy.

(Doorbell rings.)

BARBARA: That'll be Rod. Don't bother, I'll open the door.

ROD: Hello, Mrs Cooper. Hi, Jack! Excited about your journey?

PEGGY: Yes, very.

ROD: But what about the language, Mrs Cooper?

PEGGY: Well, I don't know...

JACK: Oh, she'll be all right. Peggy took evening classes in French.

PEGGY: I didn't learn much. We did grammar all the time. We didn't learn how to *speak* the language.

ROD: Don't worry! It won't be very difficult once you get there.

PEGGY: Perhaps you're right.

ROD: Right! The wine — sparkling French wine! Cheers!

BARBARA: What do they say in France?

ROD: Salut!

JACK: We say Cheers!

BARBARA: Cheers, mum! Cheers, dad! I hope you'll both be very, very happy.

ROD: Good luck!

PEGGY: Thank you, Rod. And you will come to see us, won't you? Both of you.

BARBARA: I'm sure it will be soon, won't it, Rod?

Answer:

1. Why are the Coopers celebrating?
2. Why doesn't Jack think Rod will come?
3. Why is Barbara 'alone'?
4. Does Barbara think that her mother will be unhappy in France?
5. Where did Peggy learn French?
6. Why didn't she learn much?
7. How does Peggy show that she likes Rod!
8. In Britain people often say 'Cheers!' when they drink. What do you say?
9. What do you think is going to happen to Rod and Barbara?

Set 2 Predictions

Whatever will be, will be...

I think I'm sure I'm not sure I don't think	Barbara will	marry Rod. be very successful. change her job. marry someone else.
	Rod will	go back to Canada. stay in Britain. go to the USA. marry Barbara.
	the Coopers will	like France. come home soon. miss England. make a lot of friends.

Make a prediction	*Agree positively*	*Agree neutrally*	*Disagree*
I think Barbara will marry Rod.	Yes, I'm sure she will. Yes, so do I. Yes, I do, too.	Well, maybe she will. Mm, possibly. Perhaps she will.	No, I'm sure she won't! Do you? I don't. Well, I don't think she will.
I don't think Barbara will marry Rod.	No, I'm sure she won't. Neither do I. Nor do I. I don't, either.	Well, maybe she won't. Mm, possibly not. Perhaps not.	Yes, she will! Don't you? I do. Well, I think she will.

**1. In pairs, talk about the people in this book. Make positive
   predictions and comment on them as you think, like this:**
I think Barbara will marry Rod.
Well, maybe she will.

**2. Make negative predictions and comment on them as you want,
   like this:**
I don't think Barbara will marry Rod.
No, I'm sure she won't.

**3. Write out three more predictions about the people in the book or
   about people in your class.**

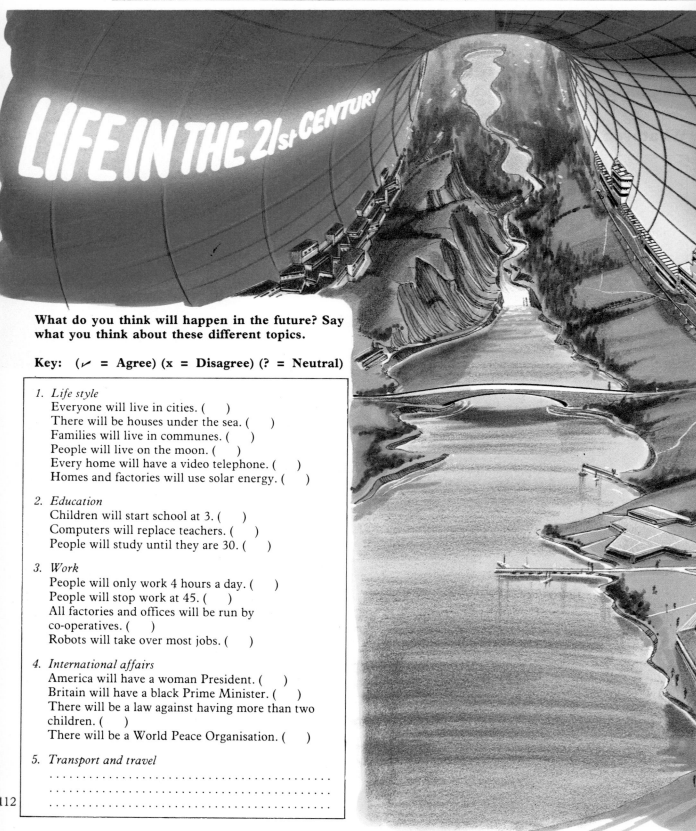

What do you think will happen in the future? Say what you think about these different topics.

Key: (✓ = Agree) (x = Disagree) (? = Neutral)

1. Life style
Everyone will live in cities. (   )
There will be houses under the sea. (   )
Families will live in communes. (   )
People will live on the moon. (   )
Every home will have a video telephone. (   )
Homes and factories will use solar energy. (   )

2. Education
Children will start school at 3. (   )
Computers will replace teachers. (   )
People will study until they are 30. (   )

3. Work
People will only work 4 hours a day. (   )
People will stop work at 45. (   )
All factories and offices will be run by
co-operatives. (   )
Robots will take over most jobs. (   )

4. International affairs
America will have a woman President. (   )
Britain will have a black Prime Minister. (   )
There will be a law against having more than two
children. (   )
There will be a World Peace Organisation. (   )

5. Transport and travel
. . . .
. . . .
. . . .

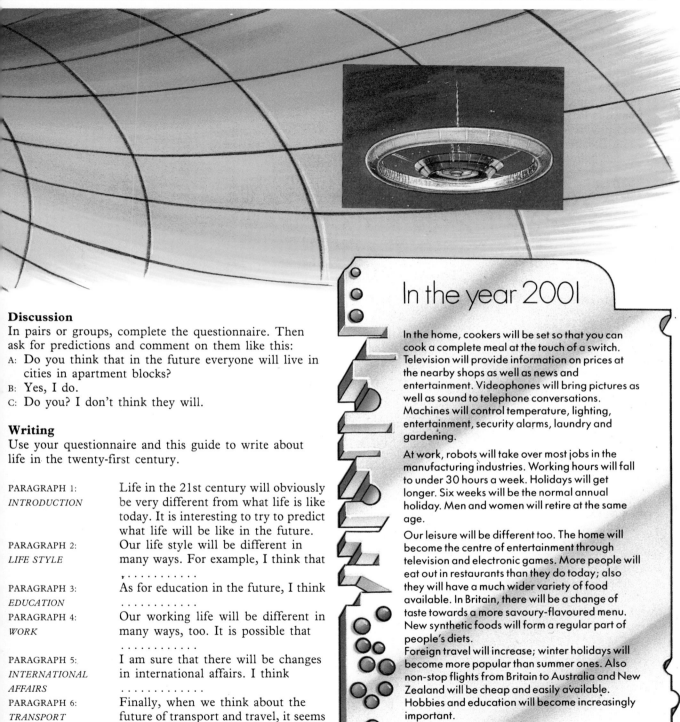

Discussion

In pairs or groups, complete the questionnaire. Then ask for predictions and comment on them like this:

A: Do you think that in the future everyone will live in cities in apartment blocks?

B: Yes, I do.

C: Do you? I don't think they will.

Writing

Use your questionnaire and this guide to write about life in the twenty-first century.

PARAGRAPH 1: *INTRODUCTION*	Life in the 21st century will obviously be very different from what life is like today. It is interesting to try to predict what life will be like in the future.
PARAGRAPH 2: *LIFE STYLE*	Our life style will be different in many ways. For example, I think that ....
PARAGRAPH 3: *EDUCATION*	As for education in the future, I think ....
PARAGRAPH 4: *WORK*	Our working life will be different in many ways, too. It is possible that ....
PARAGRAPH 5: *INTERNATIONAL AFFAIRS*	I am sure that there will be changes in international affairs. I think ....
PARAGRAPH 6: *TRANSPORT AND TRAVEL*	Finally, when we think about the future of transport and travel, it seems to me that it is quite possible that ....

In the year 2001

In the home, cookers will be set so that you can cook a complete meal at the touch of a switch. Television will provide information on prices at the nearby shops as well as news and entertainment. Videophones will bring pictures as well as sound to telephone conversations. Machines will control temperature, lighting, entertainment, security alarms, laundry and gardening.

At work, robots will take over most jobs in the manufacturing industries. Working hours will fall to under 30 hours a week. Holidays will get longer. Six weeks will be the normal annual holiday. Men and women will retire at the same age.

Our leisure will be different too. The home will become the centre of entertainment through television and electronic games. More people will eat out in restaurants than they do today; also they will have a much wider variety of food available. In Britain, there will be a change of taste towards a more savoury-flavoured menu. New synthetic foods will form a regular part of people's diets.

Foreign travel will increase; winter holidays will become more popular than summer ones. Also non-stop flights from Britain to Australia and New Zealand will be cheap and easily available. Hobbies and education will become increasingly important.

Look at the predictions and note down those that have already come true.

Unit 15

🔊 **Listening**

Listen to the report of an American diplomat's world
tour. As you listen:
a) trace his route from Washington
b) note the name of each city he will stop at
c) note the date of each stop
d) note the topics he will discuss — note the number
   from this list:

1. Food production
2. South East Asia
3. Oil and pollution
4. Sino-Indian relations
5. The space programme

Map cities: Oslo, Helsinki, Moscow, London, Paris, Bonn, Madrid, Washington, Peking, New Delhi, Rio de Janeiro, Buenos Aires

Group work

A group of Australian teenagers are coming to stay in
your town for two weeks, to get to know the people
and learn the language. First plan all the arrangements
for them. Use the agenda below and make notes of
your decisions.

1. MEETING AND ARRIVAL   We will meet the party at
                         ... on ...
2. TRANSPORT TO THEIR   A coach will ...
   ACCOMMODATION
3. ACCOMMODATION   They will stay in/at/with
                         ...
4. LANGUAGE CLASSES   They will go to classes at
                         ...
5. FREETIME ACTIVITIES   There will be some/a ...
                         at/in ... on ...
6. RETURN JOURNEY   They will travel by ... to
                         ... at ... on ...
7. OTHER DETAILS   ....

Writing

Write a letter to the leader of the group, giving details
of the arrangements. Use your notes from the
discussion, and the letter on page 108 as a guide. Start
like this:

Dear Miss Fountain,
   Here are the arrangements for
the group which is coming to stay
in July for two weeks.

Oral exercises

1. Confirm travel arrangements (1)
Will anyone meet us at the airport?
Yes, there'll be someone.
Will we get a meal on the plane?
Yes, there'll be a meal.

1. anyone meet us at the airport?
2. get a meal on the plane?
3. get a bus to the hotel?
4. anyone meet us at the hotel?
5. get any lunch at the hotel?
6. have a bath in our hotel room?

2. Confirm travel arrangements (2)
You are Freda Curtis, the Personnel Officer at
Western. Jack Cooper rings you about his trip.
Good morning, Mrs Curtis. I'm ringing about the trip
to Toulouse.

Will we have to order a taxi to the airport?
No, you won't.
And what about the check-in time? Will we have to
check-in by 8.30?
Yes, you will.

1. have to order a taxi to the airport?
2. have to check-in by 8.30?
3. be able to have more than 20 kilos of baggage each?
4. get anything to eat on the plane?
5. have a hotel in France?
6. have to find the hotel ourselves?
7. get any French money?

3. Agree with predictions (1)
I don't think Rod will stay at Western.
Nor do I.
I think he'll go back to Canada.
So do I.

1. I don't think Rod will stay at Western.
2. I think he'll go back to Canada.
3. Because I think Barbara's too independent for him.
4. You see, I don't think she'll stay in Bristol.
5. I think she'll move to London and open a shoe shop
   there.
6. So I don't think Rod will want to stay in Bristol.

4. Agree with predictions (2)
I think Jack Cooper will enjoy the job in France.
Yes, I do, too.
But I don't think Peggy will find it so easy there.
No, I don't either.

1. I think Jack Cooper will enjoy the job in France.
2. But I don't think Peggy will find it so easy there.
3. I think she'll miss her friends a bit.
4. But I think she'll learn French quite quickly.
5. But I don't think Jack will.
6. Because I think he'll speak English most of the time
   at work.

5. Agree or disagree with predictions. (Open
   exercise)
Now take Barbara, for example, She's pretty, she's
clever and she's got a good job. I think she'll be very
successful.
(Yes, so do I.)
I think she'll soon move to London.
(Oh, I don't think she will.)

1. I think Barbara will be successful.
2. I think she'll soon move to London.
3. And I think she'll never marry Rod.
4. I think she'll soon get settled down and be
   a housewife.
5. I don't think she'll combine her career and
   a family.
6. I think she'll be very content just to be a mother.

6. Question people's predictions
A friend is talking about a day trip to a seaside town.

I think it'll be fine tomorrow.
Oh? Do you really think it will?
Yes, so there'll be a lot of traffic on the roads.
Oh? Do you really think there will?
And there won't be anywhere to park in Bournemouth.
Oh, do you really think there won't?

1. fine tomorrow.
2. a lot of traffic on the roads.
3. nowhere to park in Bournemouth.
4. the beach awful.
5. so many people.
6. no place to sit down.
7. a lot of oil on the beach.
8. Look, let's stay at home. It'll be much nicer . . .

Unit 16 Consolidation

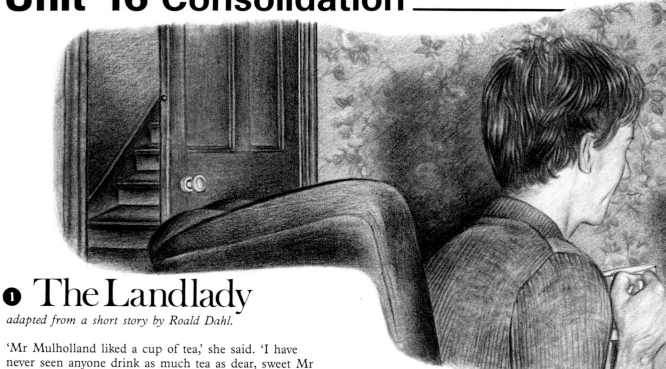

❶ The Landlady

adapted from a short story by Roald Dahl.

'Mr Mulholland liked a cup of tea,' she said. 'I have never seen anyone drink as much tea as dear, sweet Mr Mulholland. Never in my life.'

'I suppose he left quite recently,' Billy said. He was
5 still thinking about the two names. He was sure he had seen them in the newspapers.

'Left?' she said, surprised. 'But my dear boy, he never left. He's still here. Mr Temple is also here. They're on the third floor together.'

10 Billy put down his cup slowly on the table and stared at his landlady. She smiled at him, and then she put out one of her white hands and patted him on his knee. 'How old are you, my dear?' she asked.
'Seventeen.'

15 'Seventeen!' she cried. 'Oh, it's a perfect age! Mr Mulholland was also seventeen. But I think he was shorter than you are, and his teeth weren't quite so white. You have the most beautiful teeth, Mr Weaver, did you know that?'

20 'They're not as good as they look,' Billy said.
'Mr Temple, of course, was a little older,' she said. 'He was actually twenty-eight. But he didn't look twenty-eight. There wasn't a blemish on his body.'
'A what?' Billy said.

25 'A mark, my dear, there wasn't a mark. His skin was just like a baby's.'
Billy picked up his teacup and took another sip of his tea. He waited for her to say something else, but she was silent. He sat and stared into the far corner of the
30 room, biting his lower lip.
'That parrot,' he said at last. 'You know something? When I first saw it, I thought it was alive.'
'Alas, no longer.'

'It's terribly clever,' he said. 'It doesn't look the least
35 bit dead. Who did it?'
'I did.'
'You did?'
'Of course,' she said. 'And have you met my little Basil as well?'

40 She nodded towards the dachshund in front of the fire. Billy looked at it. He put out his hand and touched it on top of its back. It was cold and hard.
'Good gracious me!' he said 'How absolutely fascinating! It must be awfully difficult to do a thing
45 like that.'
'Not in the least,' she said. 'I stuff *all* my little pets myself when they die. Would you like another cup of tea?'
'No, thank you,' Billy said. The tea tasted strange—
50 faintly of bitter almonds—and he didn't like it very much.
'You signed the book, didn't you?'
'Oh, yes.'
'That's good. Because later on, if I forget your name,
55 then I can come down here and look it up. I still do that almost every day with Mr Mulholland and Mr...Mr...'
'Temple,' Billy said. 'Gregory Temple. Excuse me asking, but haven't there been any other guests here
60 except them in the last two or three years?'
Holding her teacup high in one hand, she looked at him and gave another gentle little smile.
'No, my dear,' she said. 'Only you!'

1. Text study

In the story there are many pronouns like **them, he, it, they** and **that.** Study the text and say what these pronouns refer to. Like this:

   1. *them* line 6 refers to *the two names*

   1. *them* line 6
   2. *he*   7
   3. *it*   15
   4. *they*   20
   5. *it*   32
   6. *it*   35
   7. *it*   42
   8. *that*   45
   9. *it*   50
  10. *it*   55
  11. *that*   56

2. Listening

Listen to a reading of *The Landlady* from the radio series *Stories after midnight*. Follow the text.

3. Group work

Work in pairs or small groups. Discuss these questions about the story *The Landlady.*
1. Why do you think that the 'two names' had been in the newspaper?
2. The landlady thought that Billy and the other two people were attractive. What did she like about them?
3. Why do you think there have been no other guests in the house since Mr Mulholland and Mr Temple?
4. What is the landlady's special skill?
5. What do you think is going to happen to Billy?
6. What do you think you would find upstairs in the house?
7. Would you go upstairs?

Now roleplay the dialogue between the landlady and Billy Weaver.

②

Being made redundant and finding a new job

Whatever industry you work in, and whatever your sex, age, education or family background, someone like you has lost their job in the past couple of years.

Possibilities

The first thing to do is to look at your experience, your strengths and weaknesses, likes and dislikes — and decide what sort of thing you *want* to do, and *can* do, next. In general, the possibilities are to:
- look for the same sort of job as you've done in the past.
- look for a different sort of job.
- start up your own business.
- retrain or take further education.
- move to another area.
- go abroad.
- do voluntary work.
- take vocational guidance.

Where to get help

Looking for a new job is a full-time occupation in itself, so it's important to get yourself organised.
Use as many as possible of the following sources to help you find a job:
- Jobcentre/Employment Office.
- local Careers Service.
- private employment agencies — both specialist and general.
- national and local newspapers. (It's cheaper to look at them in your local library.)
- professional or trade newspapers and journals (again, use the library).
- applications to possible employers.
- your previous employer(s)/colleagues/work contacts.
- your professional association/trade union.
- local radio stations.
- friends and relatives.

Making an application

The aim of your application is to get you an *interview;* the aim of the interview is to get you the *job.*

The first thing to do is to draw up a personal information chart or **curriculum vitae** (CV). This should contain clearly separated sections, setting out:
- personal details — full name, address, phone number, date of birth, marital status.
- your work experience, beginning with your present job and working backwards — give the dates for each post held, the organisations you worked for, a brief description of your responsibilities, and a list of your achievements in each. Don't leave out any period of time.
- your educational background — the schools and colleges you went to (with dates) and the examinations you passed. Mention any professional qualifications that you have, and any professional associations you belong to.
- details of any training.
- finally, add any personal particulars which are relevant (foreign languages, voluntary work, interests and so on).

A covering letter

You should send a short **covering letter** with your CV or form, setting out:
- the job you're applying for, and where you saw it advertised.
- how your work experience is relevant to the vacancy (read through the ad carefully).
- how your education, training or qualifications are relevant.
- why you're interested in the job.
- how available you are for interviews. Make sure that you've given your phone number.

1. Answer True or False

1. Being made redundant only happens to people over 40 with no qualifications.
2. The article is about how awful it is to be unemployed.
3. The article gives advice on what to do if you are made redundant.

2. Roleplay

Your partner has been made redundant. He/she is thinking of moving abroad. Your task is as follows:

1. Persuade him/her to stay in the country and look for a job.
2. Think of a suitable job for your partner. (Look at the list of jobs on page 14 in Unit 2) or find one in a local or national newspaper. Discuss the job with your partner and his/her qualifications for it. Persuade him/her to apply for it.
3. Help your partner to make out a CV. Ask the relevant questions under the section 'Making an application' and make notes of your partner's answers.

3. Writing

Write a curriculum vitae for yourself for the job your partner has chosen for you (see Roleplay above), or any other job you prefer. Write a covering letter to go with it.

4. Discussion

What do you think it feels like to be made redundant? Discuss this in small groups.

3 **Complete these conversational exchanges.**

1. A: ....
   B: Greece? No, never. Have you?
2. A: ....
   B: No, I haven't. I thought washing the car was your job.
3. A: ....
   B: I thought it was marvellous. I don't often go to concerts so I was quite surprised.
4. A: Why do you think a Volvo is better than a Jaguar?
   B: ....
5. A: I thought you had a job in the record shop after leaving college.
   B: ....
   A: Oh, I see. I don't know how you can study and work at the same time.
6. A: ....
   B: Ten years! I don't think I'd like to work in the same place for ten years.
7. A: When did you leave school?
   B: ....
   A: Was it so long ago? What have you been doing for the past ten years, then?
8. A: ....
   B: Since 1982. We moved from the London flat in November of 1982.
9. A: ....
   B: In 1955. He was the youngest of a family of five.
10. A: ....
    B: No, I haven't. I'm an only child.

4 **Complete the text about Jack Cooper. Put the verbs in the brackets ( ) in their right form.**

Jack Cooper (be) production manager at Western Aeronautics for ten years. He (live) in a small house in the suburbs of Bristol with his wife, Peggy. At the moment, Western (expand) into Europe and they (build) a new factory in Toulouse.

A few months ago, Jack (go) to Toulouse to look at the new factory. He (talk) to Peter Chester, managing director of Western about the new jobs there.

Jack (like) the sound of the new jobs and (think) that he would like to work in France. When he (get) back to Bristol, he (discuss) things with his wife and they (decide) to leave Bristol.

They (have) a farewell party two weeks ago. The cost of living (be) higher in France, but Western say they (provide) a house with the job — so in fact, the money Jack (earn) in Toulouse (be) better than in Bristol.

5 Fill in the correct prepositions.

1. I don't go ... work ... Saturdays or Sundays.
2. We arrived ... London ... exactly eight o'clock.
3. Come ... ten o'clock ... Friday morning.
4. He was born ... five ... the morning ... December 25th.
5. He died ... 1974.
6. The coffee is ... the blue cupboard ... the top shelf.
7. We went ... London ... car.
8. Get ... the number 33 bus and get off ... the third stop.
9. Who is John talking ...? I don't recognise her.
10. What are they talking ... ?
11. Thanks ... the lovely flowers.
12. The bus stop is ... the bottom ... the road.
13. Walk ... this road and turn left ... the traffic lights.
14. Thanks, and the same ... you.
15. I must write ... my mother.
16. I stayed ... school ... the age of 16.
17. I started work ... 17.
18. I'm staying ... friends.
19. ... dinner, I like listening ... records.
20. Let's go ... a walk ... the garden.
21. They have lived ... the same house ... ten years.
22. They got married 5 years ...
23. He's been sitting ... the library ... ten o'clock this morning.
24. ... breakfast, she washed up and made the beds.

6 Roleplay

Work in pairs. You are Mike Sanders; your partner is Rod Nelson. Interview Rod, using information from the book *and your imagination.* Use the notes below to help to prepare your interview:

When/where born?
Where grew up/lived as a child?
Family background — parents/brothers/sisters?
Education — where/how long ago?
Early career — where/first job?
How long — as electrical engineer?
           living in Bristol?
           intends to stay in Britain?
Interests — what preferences?
Recent activities — what places visited/what seen/ what done?
Opinions — Bristol/English food/English people?
Comparisons with Canada?
Predictions for future — job/life in five years' time?

7 Open dialogue

Talk to Barbara. You meet at the check-in desk at London Airport.

BARBARA: Hello, there! What a surprise! How are you?
YOU: ....
BARBARA: Anyway, what are you doing here?
YOU: ....
BARBARA: Really! Well. I'm just off to Canada. Ottawa, actually. Have you ever been there?
YOU: ....
BARBARA: Of course, you haven't heard my news.
YOU: ....
BARBARA: Well, I've got engaged. Yes! I think I'll be happy over there.
YOU: ....
BARBARA: Where do you think you'll be this time next year?
YOU: ....
BARBARA: Well, be good, won't you? Whatever you do.
YOU: ....
BARBARA: And your English is so good now. You will work hard at it, won't you?
YOU: ....
BARBARA: Well, it was nice meeting you again. Bye!
YOU: ....

8 Discussion

Work in groups. Discuss the best way to travel. Use these questions to help you start your discussion:

Have you ever travelled by plane?
Where to?
Did you enjoy it?
Did anything go wrong?
Was it better/worse than other means of transport? Why?
Which way of travelling is most comfortable? most convenient? cheapest? most inconvenient? Why?
Have you ever had any dramatic/exciting/amusing/ unusual experiences when travelling?
Is travelling becoming easier or more difficult? Why?
What will travel be like in the year 2002?

9 📼 **Listening**

Listen to the commentary from a fashion show. The commentator will say the name of each model and describe his/her clothes. Write the names of each model by each picture.

10 📼 **Listening quiz**

Make two groups: Team A and Team B.
Take turns to answer the questions.
Listen to the instructions on the tape.
Stop the tape after each question.
You will hear the right answer before you hear the next questions.
See which team answers most questions correctly.

Flight to Paradise Island

a game of chance and language strategies

RULES

1. You need: a dice, counters and 2, 3 or 4 players.
2. Each player chooses an airline with a flight number to begin the journey to Paradise Island.
   These are:
   British Airways — Flight BA 806
   Varig (Brazilian Airlines) — Flight VA 578
   Scandinavian Airlines System — Flight SK 432
   Japan Airlines — Flight JL 143
3. Each player starts from a different airport on the board and moves clockwise round the board until he lands on the correct Flight Path to Paradise Island.
4. At each stopover the player reads the Flight Report for that stopover. He/She must do two things:

   a) carry out a language function
   b) read and obey the flight instruction.
5. A player must throw the correct number to land safely on the island. The first player to reach Paradise Island is the winner. The other players can continue the game for second and third positions.
6. To start the flight, all players throw the dice once. The player with the highest number starts.

Are you ready?

Have you chosen your airport and airline?

Have you checked your flight number?

Accra: Arrange to meet the player on your right on Paradise Island. Telephone and describe what you look like. *Fly direct to Nairobi.*

Athens: Tell the player on your left why you think your airline is better. *Get on the wrong plane and go to Nandi.*

Auckland: You need to change some money. Ask about a bank. *Go back to Honolulu.*

Baghdad: Ask the air attendant for a newspaper. Name the one you would like. *Miss a turn.*

Bangkok: You've lost your suitcase. Tell the player on your right what it's like and what's in it. *Go back to Tokyo.*

Bogota: You have a headache and feel sick. Ask the air attendant for help. *Miss a turn.*

Brazilia: You forgot to close your window at home. Telephone a neighbour (player on your left) and ask for help. *You are re-routed to Honolulu.*

Budapest: Tell all the players what the weather is like today. *Fly direct to Tokyo.*

Cairo: You visit the Pyramids and lose your passport. Tell the police what happened. *Throw 6 to land on Paradise Island.*

Calcutta: Make two predictions about your future life on Paradise Island. *Fly to Ho Chi Minh City.*

Caracas: You stay at the Caracas Hilton. Ask about the facilities in the hotel. *You are re-routed to Vienna.*

Casablanca: Tell the other players about three things you did in the last place you visited. *You are re-routed to Brazilia.*

Columbo: Ask the player opposite you if he/she knows which country you are in. *If he/she knows, have another turn. If he/she doesn't know, go back to Nandi.*

Dar-es-Salaam: Ask about the beaches on Paradise Island. *Throw 6 to land.*

Djakarta: Ask any player a question about his/her educational background. *Miss a turn.*

Ho Chi Minh City: Describe where you live to the passenger (player) on your left. *Fly back to Peking to the World Table-Tennis Championship.*

Honolulu: Ask the player on your left where he/she has come from. *Invite him/her to join you in Honolulu and continue his/her journey from there.*

Kingston: Talk to the player opposite you. Suggest some things to do in your capital city. *Invite him/her to join you in Kingston and continue his/her journey from there.*

London: Flight BA 806 starts here.

Melbourne: Ask the passenger on your left if he/she would like a drink and ask the air attendant for drinks for both of you. *Miss a turn.*

Montreal: Ask the air attendant for a seat in the non-smoking part of the plane. *Fly direct to Honolulu.*

Nairobi: You photograph the wild animals. Tell the other players what equipment you have brought. *Miss a turn.*

Nandi: You go swimming and see a shark near the beach. Warn people of the danger. *Go back to Vancouver.*

Paris: You spill a drink on the passenger next to you. Apologise and offer help. *You are re-routed to Brazilia.*

Peking: You visit the Great Wall of China. Tell the other players your opinion of it. *Ask the player opposite to join you in Peking and continue his/her journey from there.*

Perth: An Australian friend has invited you to visit him. Telephone him, refuse his invitation and give an excuse. *Go back to Singapore.*

Rio de Janeiro: Flight VA 578 starts here.

Rome: The aircrew are leaving. Thank them and say goodbye. *Fly direct to Budapest.*

Singapore: Telephone all the other players and tell them about the last place you visited and what you did there. *Ask them all to join you in Singapore.*

Stockholm: Flight SK 432 starts here.

Tokyo: Flight JL 143 starts here.

Vancouver: You don't like your seat. Ask the air attendant if you can change it. *You are re-routed to Tokyo.*

Vienna: Ask the player opposite if he/she knows how to say 'Thank you' in German. *If he/she knows, you have another turn. If he/she doesn't know, miss a turn.*

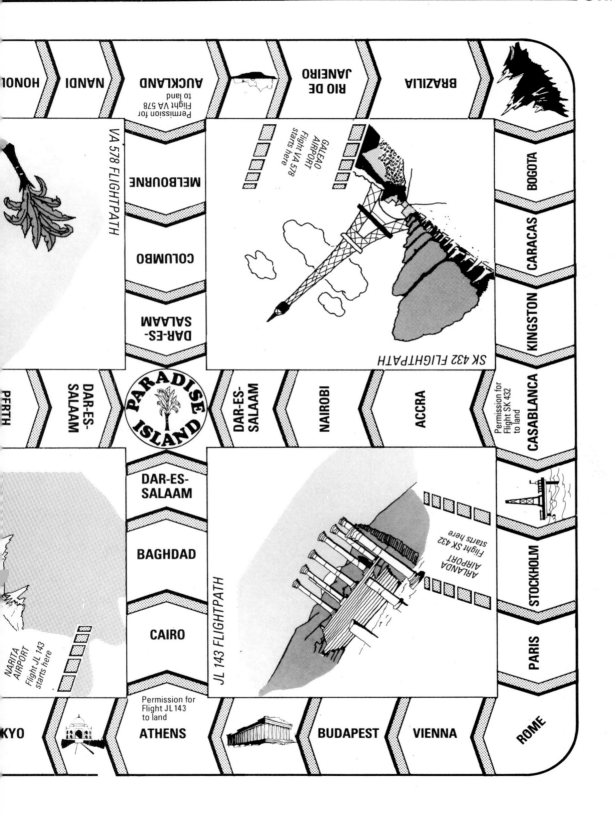

Language summaries

Unit 1 A new start

1. Ask for and give
   personal information

   Where were you born?
   I was born in Canada.
   What do you do?
   I'm an engineer.

2. Ask for and give
   geographical location

   Which part of England
   is it in?
   It's in the south-west
   –quite close to the sea.

Grammar

This is	Jack's room. the Cooper's house.

It's A friend of	mine. yours. his. hers. ours. theirs.

He	likes enjoyed	living in Bristol. meeting Barbara.

How long	have you		studied English?
	has	he she	

I've He's She's	studied English	for	one year. six months.

What	do you		do?	I'm He's She's	an engineer.
	does	he she			a cashier.

Where	do	you they	live?
	does	he she	

I They	live	in Bristol.
He She	lives	

Where	are	you they	living at the moment?
	is	he she	

I'm They're He's She's	living in London.

Where	were	you they	born?
	was	he she	

They	were		born in Canada.
I He She	was		

Western Aeronautics is a company *which* produces electrical components.
There he met Barbara *who* is Jack and Peggy's daughter.
He also likes England *because* it's so different from Canada.
Rod doesn't know many people in Bristol *so* he enjoyed meeting Barbara.

Active vocabulary and expressions

engineer	supermarket	village	to be born	northern	(It was) Nice
company	accountant	capital	study	eastern	meeting you!
manager (ess)	suburb	component	enjoy	southern	
hostel	port	spare time	produce	western	
birth	river	term	know (people)	called	
production	coast	office		based	
cashier	mountain	desk	industrial	situated	
committee	member	trade union	commercial	at the moment	
			electrical	by the way	
				another	
				close to	
				exactly	

Unit 2 Making friends

Now you can:

1. Ask and talk about likes, dislikes and preferences
2. Ask for and give opinions

3. Make suggestions and plans
4. Agree and disagree with suggestions

Do you mind getting up early?
Which do you prefer, cooking or washing up?
I prefer cooking.
What do you think of this building?
How do you like the English weather?
It's a bit depressing.
How about coming next Sunday?
Why don't we meet on Sunday?
That's a great idea!
I'm not so keen on lunch.
I'd rather have tea instead.

Grammar

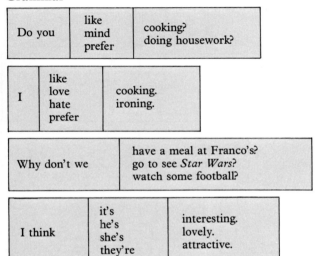

Do you	like mind prefer	cooking? doing housework?

I	like love hate prefer	cooking. ironing.

Why don't we	have a meal at Franco's? go to see *Star Wars*? watch some football?

I think	it's he's she's they're	interesting. lovely. attractive.

I don't mind	sightseeing.
I'm not so keen on	writing letters.

What How	about	having a meal at Franco's? going to see *Star Wars*? watching some football?

I'd (would) rather	have tea. go home.

I think	it he she	looks	nasty. delicious. fascinating.
	they look		

Active vocabulary and expressions

countryside	brochure	attractive	stupid	look after	besides
winter	castle	well-known	nasty	look (it looks)	actually
spring	cathedral	famous	disgusting	to be keen on	maybe
summer	captain	marvellous	good looking	would rather	so far
autumn	sense of humour	fascinating	bored	train	anyway
housework	cream	elegant	same		
story	bread	glamorous	kind	around	That's fixed.
detective	roast beef	intelligent	different	a bit	Come on.
novel	unemployment	clean	fresh	rather	It depends.
nurse (*for other*	plan	delicious		unfortunately	That's a good
jobs see p. 143)	security guard	awful	invite	yet	idea!
shift work		dull	suggest	one day	What about . . .?
uniform	friendly	unattractive	mind	together	How about . . .?
picnic	depressing	old-fashioned	prefer	on my own	To tell you the
government	light	ugly	hate	not . . . either	truth . . .
industry	ready	ordinary	dance	on the other hand	
change	romantic	untidy	iron	instead	
adventure	normal	dirty	sunbathe		125

Unit 3 Ward fifteen

Now you can:

1. Describe background to past events

It was raining.
She was walking to the village.
She slipped and fell.

2. Ask and talk about bodily health

What's the matter?
How do you feel?
I've got a pain in my back.

3. Express sympathy

Oh, I am sorry.

4. Make suggestions

Why don't you lie down?

5. Agree and disagree

Yes, so am I./No, nor am I.
Are you?/I'm not./Aren't you? I am.

6. Ask and talk about daily health routines in the past

Did you do any exercises yesterday?
What did you do yesterday?
I got up early and went swimming.

7. Ask and talk about the recent past

What did you do?
I went to see a friend.

Grammar

| How | do | you | feel today? |
| | does | he
she | |

| I've
He's
She's | got | a bad cold.
a temperature.
a pain in my/his/her back. |
| | | earache.
toothache. |

| It | was | raining | when | he | slipped. |
| She | | walking | | she | fell. |

| What | was | he
she | doing | when the gas exploded? |
| | were | you
they | | |

| My | head
throat | feels | hot.
sore. |
| | legs | feel | weak. |

| I | feel | sick. |
| He
She | feels | awful.
ill. |

| Why don't you | lie down?
go home?
see a doctor? |

| What did | you
he
she
they | do?
see?
have? |

| I
He
She
They | went for a walk.
saw an old film on television.
had a glass of milk. |

| So | am | I. |
| Nor | did | |

| Are
Aren't | you? | I | 'm not.
am. |
| Did
Didn't | | | didn't.
did. |

| Did you | have sugar in your tea?
do your exercises? | Yes, I did.
No, I didn't. |

Active vocabulary and expressions

lady	cold (*for other*	rolls	surprise	skate	local	amateur
widow	*illnesses see p. 143*)	crowd		stand	serious	
accident	face (*for parts of the*	shower	slip	shout	slight	alone
store	*body see p. 143*)	ice	fall	hug	glad	by chance
hip	aspirin	couple	break	agree	sick	still
farmer	sugar	mark	pass	spoil	ill	first
tractor	lump	result	explode	cheer	tired	as (= because)
farm	spoonful	score	snore	wear	sore	
ambulance	piece	insurance	feel		weak	Oh dear!
gas	toast	teenager	hurt		energetic	Give them
operation	sweet	hobby	lie down		healthy	my love!
pain	alcohol	expenses	go for a run		perfect	
back	exercise	competition	relax		quiet	
126 temperature	window	bill	try		shy	

Unit 4 Two suburbs

Now you can:

1. Ask and talk about facilities

Is there a swimming pool in Portland?
Yes, there is.
Is there a post office near here?
Yes, there's one in Elm Street.

2. Ask for and give exact locations

Where exactly is Lloyd's Bank?
It's in Elm Street between the post office and the chemist's.

3. Ask for and give directions

How do I get to the hamburger restaurant in Elm Street?
Turn right into Elm Street and it's at the end of the street on the left.

Grammar

Is	there	a chemist	here?
Are		any restaurants	

Yes,	there	is. are.
No,		isn't. aren't.

There's one	at the	beginning end	of the street.
There are two	on the corner		

There's There are	no	cinemas	in Sutton.
There aren't	any	cinemas	

There	is a pub are two banks	in Oak Street.

As well as	a cinema	there is a pub. there are two banks.
Except for		there is no other form of entertainment. there aren't any entertainment facilities.

Active vocabulary and expressions

greengrocer's (*for other shops and buildings see p. 143*)
traffic lights
corner
(a) right
duty
society
population
entertainment
facility
service
politician
speech
promise
party (political)
advice

vote
election
turning
beginning
end
square

realise
park
satisfy
cross

essential
empty
broken

as well as
except for
belong to
between
as far as

right
well (planned)
badly (planned)
left
half-way down

You can't miss it.
You're welcome.

Unit 5 A place of my own

Now you can:

1. Link events in the past — *When he saw the advertisement, he telephoned immediately.*

2. Ask for permission formally — *May I use your phone?*
Do you mind if I use your phone?
Is it all right if I use your phone?

3. Ask for permission informally — *Can I use your phone?*

4. Give permission formally — *Yes, certainly./Yes, of course.*

5. Give permission informally — *Yes, do./Yes, sure.*

6. Refuse permission formally — *Well, actually . . .*

7. Refuse permission informally — *Sorry, but . . .*

8. Describe your home and furniture — *There are three rooms upstairs.*
In my bedroom, there's a bed a desk and a lamp.
A large, blue cotton tablecloth.

Grammar

May Can Do you mind if Is it all right if	I	use your phone? close the door? turn off the TV?	Yes, of course/certainly. Yes, sure./Yes, do. Well, actually, . . . Sorry, but . . .

What's it made of?		It's made of	plastic. leather. glass. a soft material.

When he saw it, he	went home. telephoned Rod. told his parents.	A soft light blue A large leather An old, black and white checked A round glass	carpet. chair. sofa. table.

Active vocabulary and expressions

advertisement	chapter	leather	turn on	comfortable	pink	immediately
permission	volume	glass	turn off	exciting	beige	straightaway
self-service	problem	material	expect	personal	plain	upstairs
key	roof	smile	service	high	flowery	downstairs
rent	ceiling	murderer	return	low	striped	elderly
balcony	wall	lavatory	climb	hard	checked	lonely
blinds	cooker	income tax	join	soft	round	
guest	(for furniture	courage	refuse	heavy	oval	Make up your mind.
compartment	and fittings			light	rectangular	against the rules
rule	see p. 143)	serve	cheap	dark	square	
sign	floor	rent	fair	light	charming	
amplifier	wood	own	noisy	purple	magic	
call	metal	afford	freezing	grey	harmless	
regards	plastic	share	exhausted	orange	bad-tempered	

Unit 6 Consolidation

Active vocabulary and expressions

sample	lolly	sky	enjoyable	strange	most	surprisingly
adult	majority		ideal		almost	
list	open air	guess	true		nearly	according to

Unit 7 Guests for supper

Now you can:

1. Ask and talk about availability (of household provisions)
2. Ask and talk about location (of household utensils)
3. Make polite requests
4. Give instructions and advice

Have we got any milk?
We haven't got any cheese.
Where are the cups?
They're in the cupboard on the top shelf.
Could you get me some milk, please?
Don't lie in the sun for hours.
You shouldn't lie in the sun for hours.
Keep your money safe.
You should keep your money safe.

Grammar

| Have | you we they | got any | coffee? |
| Has | he she | | bread? |

| I We You They | haven't | got any | tea. wine. |
| He She | hasn't | | lemon. |

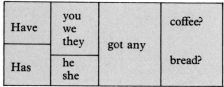

| I've He's She's We've You've They've | got | some lots of | milk. |

| On In | the | top middle bottom | shelf. drawer. |

| On the shelf in the cupboard | under above beside at the top of | the . . . |

| Could you | give get | me him her us them | another cup of tea, please? |

| You | should | put all your money | in a safe place. |
| | shouldn't | | in your pocket. |

| Put | | your money | in a safe place. |
| Don't put | | | in your pocket. |

Active vocabulary and expressions

ham (*for other food see p. 143*)	knife	commonsense	cut	chill	straight	under
shelf	fork	rate of exchange	get	sprinkle	boiling	above
recipe	spoon	tablespoon	steal	chop	extra	on top of
bowl	drawer	sheet	lock		tinned	through
diet	middle	towel	carry	cool		
cup	top	blanket	cash	bottom	as well	anything
saucer	beach	vacuum cleaner	sign	lively	finely	lots of
plate	travellers'		peel	easy-going	possibly	
saucepan	cheque		cook	miserable		Hope you have
	passport		mix	broke = (no money)	until	a good time!
					beside	

129

Unit 8 Excuses

Now you can:

1. Ask if you are interrupting
2. Explain present activities
3. Invite people to do things
4. Accept invitations

Am I disturbing you?
Am I ringing at a bad time?
I'm just washing my hair.

Would you like to come to my party?
Yes, I'd love to. That would be lovely.
I'd like to come very much.

5. Refuse invitations politely
6. Give excuses

7. Accept excuses

That's very kind of you, but I'm afraid I . . .
I'm afraid I ought to/have got to/have to do some work.
I'd like to wash my hair.
OK. Some other time.

Grammar

What's	he she	doing?
What are	you they	

He's She's I'm They're We're	having lunch. watching television. having a shower.

Do you mind I don't mind I hate	people someone	phoning disturbing calling	you me	when	you're I'm	in a meeting. (?) making supper. (?) putting the children to bed. (?)

Would you like to	go for a meal? go to the club? come to a party?

Yes, I'd love to.
That would be lovely.
Thank you. I'd like to very much.
I'd love to, but I'm afraid I . . .

I You He/She We They	ought 'd like have	to	go to bed early. stay at home tonight. write some letters.

I've You've He's/She's We've They've	got to	do the washing. make a telephone call. go to bed early.
	got a	bad cold. headache.

Active vocabulary and expressions

problem
baby
shower
card
invitation
youth club
test

entertain
feed
paint
put somebody to bed
shave
have one's hair cut
disturb
interrupt
definitely
accept

make (a phone call)
wait for
refuse

busy
bad (=inconvenient)
fun
previous

later on
for once
something

So you are!
Have a nice evening!
See you around!
That would be lovely!

That's very kind of you.
Some other time.

Unit 9 Future plans

Now you can:

1. Ask and talk about plans
2. Respond to plans
3. Remind people to do things

Where are you going to stay?
We're going to stay with friends.
Really? How lovely!
That sounds fun!
You'll remember to lock the door, won't you?
You won't forget to lock the door, will you?

4. Confirm that you will
5. Ask and talk about the weather

Yes, I will. Don't worry!
No, I won't. Don't worry!
What's the weather like in Italy?
Lovely. It's sunny and warm. It's 15 degrees centigrade.

Grammar

Where What How When How long	are	you they	going to	go? do? travel?
	is	he she		leave? spend there?

I'm He's She's We're They're	going to	(go to) Spain. lie on a beach. travel by boat and train. leave in half an hour. spend a fortnight there.

You'll remember	to close the windows,	won't you?
You won't forget		will you?

Yes, I will.
No, I won't.

Before she	left, phoned, locked up,	she	talked to Gerry. went to the bank. checked the till.

I'm leaving in	ten minutes. a quarter of an hour. three quarters of an hour. an hour.

Active vocabulary and expressions

future	day nursery	increase	already
appointment	treatment	reduce	abroad
trade	budget	improve	on average
publicity	inflation	protect	
apartment block	cost of living	reply	during
view	enemy		till
design	attack	pretty	
choice	idea	professional	have a word with
season	pocket	brand-new	
branch	taxpayer	airy	
decisions	economy	bare	
guest house		remarkable	
youth hostel	give up	second-hand	
camping site	enquire	fashionable	
fortnight	notice	wide	
fire	laugh	sunny	
seat-belt	take off	foggy	
interview	explain	windy	
degree	turn out	cloudy	
centigrade	develop	stormy	
aim	check	angry	
	cancel	fair	
	fasten	nuclear	
	snow		
	freeze		

131

Unit 10 Getting up to date

Now you can:

1. Ask about and give personal news	*Where are you living now?* *I'm living in Bristol.*
2. Check facts	*Your name's Clive, isn't it?* *You work in Madrid, don't you?*
3. Confirm facts	*That's right. It is.* *That's right. I do.*

4. Correct facts	*No, it isn't, actually.* *No, I don't, actually.*
5. Make and respond to farewells and seasonal greetings	*Have a nice evening!* *Thanks, I will.* *Merry Christmas!* *Thanks, and the same to you.* *Don't work too hard!*

Grammar

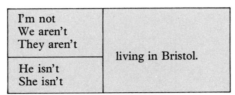

Are	you they	living in Bristol?
Is	he she	

I'm not We aren't They aren't	living in Bristol.
He isn't She isn't	

He She	was	Italian,	wasn't	he? she?
They	were	Spanish,	weren't	they?

That's right,	he she	was.
	they were.	

You're They're	English,	aren't	you? they?
He's She's It's		isn't	he? she? it?

Yes, that's right,	I am. they are	
	he she it	is.

Have a	nice	time! evening! weekend! Christmas!
	lovely	

Don't	work too hard! drive too fast! forget to write! worry!

You They	work	in Bristol,	don't	you? they?
He She	works		doesn't	he? she?

Yes,	I they	do.
	he she	does.

You	've lived	in France,	haven't you?
	lived		didn't you?

Yes, I have. No, I haven't.
Yes, I did. No, I didn't.

Active vocabulary and expressions

journalist (*for other jobs see p. 143*)
copy
prize
degree (education)
oil rig
building firm
sociology
gun

military service
general
moon
illness
wage claim
project
relationship
overtime

do well
catch (train)
become
expect (baby)
flow
believe in
land
discover
invent
fly

investigate
forgive
choose
settle down

freelance

up to date

extremely
seriously

That's a pity.
Give my regards to . . .
Look after yourself.
Merry Christmas!
Happy Easter!
The same to you.

It was nice meeting you.
Heavens!
Look at the time!
I must rush.
Give my love to . . .
Have a nice time!
Enjoy yourself!
Be good!

Unit 11 Consolidation

Active vocabulary and expressions

tobacco
small
lawyer
organisation
avocado
budget
rent
insurance
tax
electricity
gas
oil
fee
expenses
pocket money
equipment
scissors
plug
socket

put away
touch
to be on (of electric current)
challenge

sharp
to be over (= finished)
qualified
skilled
helpful

Unit 12 Home again

1. Make apologies and give explanations — *Sorry I didn't telephone you but I forgot.*
2. Make comparisons — *Milan is bigger than I expected.*
   Florence is more beautiful than Milan.
3. Agree and disagree — *Yes, that's true. Yes, I agree.*
   No, I don't agree.
4. Ask and talk about experiences — *Have you ever been to India? Yes, I have./No, never.*
5. Ask and talk about impressions — *How did you get on? We had a marvellous time.*

Grammar

Scotland France	is	colder livelier more beautiful	than	England. Spain.

The	hotel place food	was much	more less	expensive interesting exciting	than	I	thought. expected.

Before After	checking in her luggage	he she they	bought a magazine. boarded the plane.

While	he she	was	waiting, looking,	the driver he she	collected his/her luggage. had a cup of coffee.

When	she he the plane	arrived, stopped,	she he the passengers	began to relax. got off.

Have you ever	been to Spain? eaten Indian food? done any fishing?	Yes, I have once. No, never.

Active vocabulary and expressions

luggage	seaweed	miss (train)	out of date	relaxing	nervous
stone	ghost	oversleep	thin	comfortable	clear
timetable	purse	windsurf	tall	well-paid	wet
skyscraper	fare	camp	high	rewarding	crowded
career	passport control	slow down	short	sociable	
social worker	security	check in	long	difficult	more
aerobics	departure lounge	board	wide	snobbish	less
jogging	exit	take off	deep	fattening	sadly
earth	emergency	land	narrow	whole	
canal	relief		mild	heavy	Welcome back!
snail	calculator		cool	unusual	What a surprise!
garlic		tiring	lively	raw	It's lovely to see you
hang-gliding		noisy	fat	supernatural	again.
		slow			Forget it!

Unit 13 Mandy is missing

Now you can:

1. Ask about and narrate past events

   What time did you get up?
   I got up at 7.30.
   What did you do?

2. Ask about and describe people's appearance

   What does she look like?
   She's got fair hair.
   What's she wearing?
   She's wearing a raincoat.

3. Ask and talk about completed actions

   Have you asked the neighbours?
   Yes, I've just asked them.

Grammar

I've He's She's We've You've They've	got	fair dark long short	hair.

I'm He's She's	wearing	a red sweater. black boots. a raincoat.

I You We They	have('ve) haven't	finished the homework. watched TV this week. bought any oranges. written the letter.
He She	has('s) hasn't	just telephoned the police.

Have	you they	been to the theatre this week? played football recently? seen *ET* yet?
Has	he she	

Yes,	I	have.
	he	has.
No,	they	haven't.
	she	hasn't.

Active vocabulary and expressions

ribbon
tights (*for other clothes see p. 143*)
canal
engine
bank
luck
bunch
plait
ponytail

expect
play truant
worry
climb
pick

float
unplug

wild
missing
urgent
short-sleeved
long-sleeved
sleeveless
wavy
curly
straight

as soon

Unit 14 Star

Now you can:

1. Ask and talk about past events (concerning point and duration of time)

   When was he born?
   In 1935.
   How long did he go to school for?
   For seven years.
   How long have you lived here?
   I've lived here since 1979.
   I've been working here since last year.

2. Ask and talk about biographical details (in chronological order)

   Where were you born?
   Where did you grow up?
   Where did you go to school?

Grammar

When / Where	were	you	born?
	was	he / she	

I / He / She	was born	in 1958. twenty years ago. in Cardiff.

I We You They	have	been living in Cardiff	since 1965. for 14 years.
He She	has		

How long	have you been	living here?
Where		working?

That was when he	was born. died.

Marie Curie, *who* was a famous French physicist, was born in 1867.

When Why For how long	did	you she he	go to university?

Active vocabulary and expressions

concert	morals	put in prison	constantly
performance	attitudes	ban	on trial
press	civilization	search	
docks	atom bomb	force	for
price	heroine	suffer	since
peace	apartheid	punish	ago
composer	movement	bring up (a child)	against
customs officer	marriage		without
novelist	prison	successful	
miner	slave	private	
gymnastics	law	several	
medal	agriculture	poor	
box	justice	religious	
twin	playwright	typical	
talent	ballerina		
truck driver		professionally	
generation	manage	originally	
	combine	particularly	
	earn		

Unit 15 And tomorrow. . . ?

Now you can:

1. Ask and talk about travel arrangements

How will I get to the airport?
A representative will meet you.

2. Make predictions

I think Rod will leave England.
I don't think Rod will marry Barbara.

3. Agree positively

Yes, so do I./No, nor do I.
Yes, I'm sure he will.
No, I'm sure he won't.

4. Agree neutrally

Maybe she will/won't.
Perhaps (not)./Possibly (not).

5. Disagree with predictions

Do you? I don't./Don't you? I do.
Well, I don't think she will.

Grammar

How will	I you we	get to the airport? find the hotel?

A car A representative	will	fetch you. meet us.

Will Won't	you he she	miss your friends? come back to England?

I think I don't think I'm sure	it'll	rain tomorrow. happen. be fine next summer.

Oh,	do don't	you?

Yes,	I do, too. So do I.

No,	I don't, either. neither do I. nor do I.

Yes,	I she he	will. won't.
No,		

Active vocabulary and expressions

application	moon	apply	satisfactory
gate	video	enclose	pleasant
representative	solar energy	bother	atomic
currency	pet	celebrate	nearby
lift	weapon	replace	normal
snack	switch	run (= manage)	savoury
courier	sound	destroy	electronic
row	security	control	synthetic
grammar	wallpaper	retire	regular
life style	robot	increase	
commune	hobby		

Unit 16 Consolidation

Active vocabulary and expressions

almond	stuff	silent	full-time	dramatic
mark	sip	dead	relevant	unusual
interview	hold	fascinating	available	
	mention	bitter	redundant	absolutely
stare	leave out	gentle	comfortable	
pat	pass (exam)	further	convenient	
nod	realise	voluntary	amusing	

Grammatical summary_____

This summary includes items which appear in Opening Strategies and Starting Strategies as well as Building Strategies. Thus, 'OS and 9:1' means this item was first introduced in Opening Strategies but is recycled in Unit 9 Set 1 in Building Strategies. The reference will show first the Unit number and then the section in which the item first occurs.
eg: 1 = Set 1 Dial = Dialogue R = Reading text OE3 = Oral Exercise 3.

GRAMMATICAL ITEM	EXAMPLE	UNIT:SET
1. SENTENCE TYPES		
1. Declarative		OS
2. Interrogative:		OS
Yes/No questions		
Wh-questions		1:1
3. Imperative (See		
Verbs: other forms)		
4. Short answers:		
verb *to be* (present and		OS
past simple)		
have	*Yes, I have./No, I haven't.*	12:3
will	*Yes, he will./No, he won't.*	15:2
5. Echoed questions:		
past simple	*Oh, did you?*	3:3
present	*Oh, are you?*	9:OE1
6. Question tags	*You aren't English, are you?*	10:2
	You live in Bristol, don't you?	10:2
	You'll remember to lock the door, won't you?	9:2
7. Simple sentences		OS,SS
8. Compound sentences	*Rod likes Jack and enjoys his job.*	OS,SS
	He lives in a hostel but wants to rent a flat.	OS,SS
	He doesn't know many people so he enjoyed meeting her.	1:R
9. Complex sentences:		
Adverbial clauses		
of time	*When he saw it, he telephoned Rod.*	5:R
	That was when he died.	14:OE5
	While she was waiting, she had a cup of coffee.	12:R
	Wait until they cool.	7:Dial
	We'll let you know as soon as we find her.	13:Dial
	Before she left for Italy, she talked to Gerry.	9:Dial
of place	*That's where I wrote the song.*	14:Dial
of cause	*He likes England because it's so different.*	1:R
2. VERBS: MAIN TENSES		
Present tense *to be*		OS,SS
There is/There are	*There's a launderette in Oak Street.*	4:1
Present simple	*I work for IBM.*	OS,SS and 1:1
Present continuous	*At the moment I'm living in London.*	1:1, 8:1
	He's living in Madrid.	10:1
Past tense *to be*		SS
Past simple	*She slipped and fell.*	OS and 3:1
	After leaving school, I went to college.	14:2
Past simple with *ago*	*I left college four years ago.*	14:1

Past continuous	*It was raining.*	3:1
	While she was waiting, she had a coffee.	12:R
Pres. perfect simple:	*We've got some potatoes.*	7:1
	Have you closed the windows?	OS and 13:3
with *ever*	*Have you ever eaten Chinese food?*	12:3
with *yet*	*I'm afraid I haven't finished it yet.*	OS and 12:OE
with *just*	*I've just finished it.*	12:OE
Pres. perfect continuous:		
with *for*	*I've been living in Bristol for three months.*	14:1
with *since*	*I've been working here since September.*	14:1
Future:		
be going to	*I'm going to spend three weeks there.*	OS and 9:1
will	*I'll ring back later.*	8:1
	The driver will have your tickets.	15:1
	I don't think he'll stay at Western.	15:2

3. VERBS: OTHER FORMS

Imperatives:		
in commands	*Listen and repeat./Work in pairs.*	OS,SS
in instructions	*Walk down this street.*	OS and 4:2
in advice	*Put all sharp knives away.*	OS and 7:3
	Don't leave the iron on.	OS and 7:3
Conditionals		
with permission	*Do you mind if I open the window?*	5:1
Gerunds after verbs:		
enjoy	*. . . so he enjoyed meeting her.*	1
like	*I like cooking.*	OS and 2:1
hate	*I hate washing up.*	OS and 2:1
mind	*I don't mind doing homework.*	2:1
love	*I love gardening.*	2:1
prefer	*I prefer cooking to washing up.*	2:1
go	*She went swimming.*	OS and 3:Dial
Gerunds after		
prepositions:		
after	*After checking in her luggage . . .*	12:R
before	*Before going through customs . . .*	12:R
about	*How/What about going to the cinema?*	2:3
for	*Apologise for being late.*	12:1
to	*She's looking forward to getting home.*	12:R
on	*I'm not so keen on having lunch.*	2:3
Infinitives with *to* with		
auxiliaries and modals:		
going to	*I'm going to travel by air.*	OS and 9:1
ought to	*I ought to wash my hair.*	8:3
have got to	*I've got to do my washing.*	8:3
have to	*I have to do my washing.*	8:3
with main verbs:		
want	*What do you want to do?*	OS
would like	*Would you like to go out for a meal?*	OS and 8:2
decide	*He decided to find someone to share the flat.*	5:R
remember	*You'll remember to lock the doors, won't you.*	9:2
with predicative adjectives:		
sorry	*I was sorry to hear that . . .*	10:R
lovely	*It's lovely to see you again.*	12:Dial
Indirect speech	*I think it's beautiful.*	2:3
	They say it's warm and sunny.	9:Dial
	Tell them it's urgent.	13:Dial
Negative questions	*Why don't we meet for lunch?*	2:3
	Would you like to go out for a meal?	8:OE3

4. VERBS: MODALS AND AUXILIARIES

be (See Verbs: main tenses present continuous, past continuous)		
be (with inversion).	*So am I./Nor am I.*	3:3
have (See Verbs: main tenses present perfect)		
do (auxiliary)	*Do you like . . .?*	OS,SS
do (with inversion)	*So do I./Nor do I.*	OS and 15:2
	So did I./Nor did I.	3:3
can (permission)	*Can I use your telephone?*	OS,SS and 5:1
could (request)	*Could you get me some fruit, please?*	7:2
may (permission)	*May I use the bathroom?*	5:1
be going to	*I'm going to spend three weeks there.*	OS and 9:1
must (obligation)	*I must go now.*	OS,SS
ought to	*I ought to go to bed early.*	8:3
have got to	*I've got to do my washing.*	8:3
have to	*I have to do my washing.*	8:3
shall (suggestion)	*Shall we buy her some flowers?*	OS,SS
will (arrangement)	*The driver will have your tickets.*	15:1
will (prediction)	*I'm sure it will be hot.*	15:2
will (order)	*You'll remember to lock the door, won't you?*	9:2
would (offer)	*Would you like a cup of tea?*	OS,SS
would (invitation)	*Would you like to come out for a drink?*	OS and 8:2
would rather	*I'd rather go home instead.*	2:3
should (obligation)	*You should keep your money safe.*	7:3

5. VERBS: SEMI-COPULAS

feel	*I feel awful.*	3:1
look	*I think she looks attractive.*	2:2
sound	*That sounds interesting.*	9:1

6. VERBS: VOICE

Active		OS,SS
Passive	*It is situated in Bristol.* (set phrase)	1:2
	It is made of glass. (set phrase)	5:2
	I was born in England.	1:1

7. NOUNS

Number: singular and plural		
Genitive *'s*	*This is Jack's office.*	1:OE4
	At the Cooper's house.	OS and 1:R
Countable/uncountable nouns	*I'd like a/I'd like some . . .*	OS,SS
Attributive e.g. of material	*a glass table*	5:2

8. ADJECTIVES

Attributive/predicative		OS,SS
Comparatives	*I'm much better, thanks.*	3:Dial
	Canada is bigger than China.	12:2
	Florence is more beautiful than Paris.	12:2
Superlatives	*Where is the nearest post office?*	5:2
	Which is the most convenient way of travelling?	16
Qualities	*red walls/an oval table/the large cupboard/a plastic bag*	5:2
Order	*A large brown leather sofa.*	5:2

9. ADVERBS

Frequency	*He usually walks to work.*	OS,SS
Degree	*very*	OS,SS
	a lot/quite/rather/a bit	OS and 2:1

much	*I like it very much.*	OS and 2:2
Manner	*I'm very well, thank you.*	OS,SS
	Do you mind getting up early?	2:2
	He's working very hard.	10:R

10. ARTICLES

Definite/Indefinite	*the/a/an*	SS
No article	*He has lunch at one o'clock.*	SS19
	He has lunch at work.	SS19
	in summer, in winter	2:1

11. PRONOUNS

Personal (subject and object forms)		OS,SS
Impersonal	*You turn first left.*	4:2
Possessives:		
adjectives	*his, her, my, your, etc.*	OS,SS
pronouns	*That's yours, over there.*	OS and 1:OE3
Demonstratives:		
pronouns	*That is the bathroom and that's the kitchen.*	OS,SS
adjectives	*I'd like these/those apples, please.*	OS,SS
Distributive	*I like everything.*	OS,SS
Quantitative		
one	*Which one would you like?*	OS,SS
some/any	*We've got some onions.*	OS and 7:1
	We haven't got any mayonnaise.	
no	*There are no cinemas here.*	4:1
someone	*We found someone for the upstairs flat.*	3:Dial
something	*Would you like something to eat?*	7:R
anyone	*Will anyone meet us?*	15:1
anything	*Have we got anything to eat?*	7:1
nobody	*Nobody has seen her.*	13:Dial
nothing	*It costs nothing.*	SS
many	*Many people come to live in England.*	OS,SS
lots of	*We've got lots of potatoes.*	7:1
Interrogative adverbs:		
Who (object)	*Who did you see?*	3:OE6
What	*What time is it?*	OS,SS
	What colour is it?	OS and 5:2
	What's the weather like?	OS and 9:3
Which	*Which part of England is it in?*	OS and 1:2
Interrogative adverbs:		
When/Where/How		OS,SS
How many/How much		
How long/How far	*How long have you studied English for?*	1:R
How often		
Why	*Why did he leave Canada?*	OS and 2:R
Relatives:		
which	*. . . a small company which makes electrical components.*	1:R
who	*There he met Barbara who is Jack and Peggy's daughter.*	1:R
Emphatic	*I'm expecting a call myself.*	5:1

12. PREPOSITIONS

Place:	*next to, near, opposite, in front of, behind, in, at, outside*	SS,OS
	from, to, past, without, in, on, under, above, beside, into	7:2
	between, across, at the end of, at the beginning of, in	
	the middle of, off, as far as, on the other side of	4:2
Time:	*at, on, in*	OS,SS
	for, since	1:R, 14:1
	before, after	OS,SS and 3:3

Instrument
    by   *by car*   OS,SS
    in   *We'll go in the company car.*   15:1

13. MISCELLANEOUS

    as well as   *As well as a swimming pool, there is also an athletics*
                                      stadium.   4:R
    except for   *Except for a cinema, there is no other form of*
                                        entertainment.   4:R

Vocabulary

Note: the numbers refer to the unit of Building Strategies in which the word appears.

Jobs and professions

actor	2
actress	2
airline steward	2
architect	2
carpenter	10
cashier	9
composer	14
computer operator	2
customs officer	14
designer	10
diver	13
electrician	3
folk singer	14
hairdresser	2
judge	3
language teacher	10
librarian	10
manager	1
manageress	1
miner	14
novelist	14
nurse	2
personnel officer	15
policeman	2
pop star	14
representative	2
social worker	12
travel guide	2

Ailments and illnesses

appendicitis	
asthma	
chicken pox	
cold	3
cough	3
earache	3
German measles	
glandular fever	
hay fever	
headache	3
influenza	3
measles	
mumps	
pain	3
sore throat	3
stomachache	3
temperature	3
toothache	3
whooping cough	

Parts of the body

ankle	3
arm	3
ear	3
elbow	3
eye	3
face	3
finger	3
foot	3
hand	3
head	3
knee	3
leg	3
mouth	3
neck	3
nose	3
shoulder	3
stomach	3
throat	3
thumb	3
toe	3
tooth	3
wrist	3

Public buildings, places and shops

airport	15
athletics stadium	4
baker's	4
bank	4
bar	OS
bookshop	OS
boutique	OS
bus station	4
butcher's	4
café	OS
car park	4
cathedral	4
chemist's	OS
church	OS
cinema	OS
college	OS
comprehensive school	3
department store	OS
dry cleaner's	4
embassy	OS
factory	OS
fish and chip shop	4
football ground	
garage	4
greengrocer's	4
hairdresser's	4
hospital	4
hostel	9
hotel	4
jeweller's	OS
lake	4
launderette	4
library	4
museum	4
newsagent's	5
night club	4
petrol station	4
pizza bar	OS
playground	
police station	OS
post office	OS
pub	OS
railway station	4
restaurant	OS
school	OS
shopping centre	OS
stationer's	OS
supermarket	OS
swimming pool	4
taxi rank	OS
tennis court	4
theatre	OS
toy shop	OS
travel agency	4
university	4

Furniture and fittings

armchair	5
banisters	
bidet	
bookcase	5
carpet	5
central heating	5
chair	OS
cooker	5
cupboard	5
curtain	5
desk	5
drawer	7
dressing table	
freezer	5
fridge	5
front door	5
lamp	5
picture	5
shelf	7
sink	5
sofa	5
table	OS
toilet	OS
wardrobe	5
washbasin	5

Food

apple	7
bean	7
bread	7
butter	7
cheese	7
chicken	11
cornflakes	7
cream	11
egg	7
fish	7
flour	7
fruit	7
ham	7
jam	7
lemon	7
lettuce	7
milk	7
mushroom	11
onion	7
orange	7
prawn	11
strawberry	11
tomato	7

Clothes and accessories

bag	OS
belt	13
blouse	13
boots	13
bracelet	
cardigan	13
coat	13
dress	13
jacket	13
jeans	OS
jewellery	
pullover	
raincoat	13
running shoes	OS
sandals	
shirt	13
shoes	OS
skirt	OS
socks	
stockings	
sweater	OS
sweatshirt	OS
tie	OS
tights	OS
tracksuit	13
trainers	13
trousers	13
T-shirt	OS
umbrella	OS
underwear	
waistcoat	

Longman Group UK Limited
Longman House
Burnt Mill
Harlow
Essex
England

© Brian Abbs and Ingrid Freebairn 1984

First published 1984
Twelfth impression 1987
ISBN 0-582-57945-7

The publishers would like to point out that all characters in the book are completely fictitious.

Printed in Spain by Tonsa, San Sebastian.

Acknowledgements
We are grateful to the following for permission to reproduce copyright photographs:

All Sport Photographic Ltd. for page 25; Art Directors Photo Library for page 77 (top); Barnaby's Picture Library for pages 8 (bottom right), 16 (top right), and 69 (top right); British Tourist Authority for page 69 (middle right); Reproduced with permission of The Broxbourne School for page 74-75 (top); Ray Halin/Camera Press London for page 8 (top left) and Camera Press London for page 106; The J. Allan Cash Photo Library for pages 69 (bottom right), 72-73 and 74 (bottom left); Terence le Goubin/Colorific! for page 68 (middle) and Earl Young/Colorific! for page 69 (top left); Colour Library International for pages 8 (bottom left), 16 (top left), 17 (middle left) and 45; Crown Copyright, reproduced with the permission of the Controller of Her Majesty's Stationery Office for page 67 (middle); Cumbernauld Development Corporation for page 32 (left); Djukanovic/Daily Telegraph Colour Library for page 17 (top left) and Steve Back/Daily Telegraph Colour Library for page 69 (bottom left); Elizabeth Whiting & Associates for page 16 (bottom left); The photographs of Elvis Presley on pages 104-105 are from the exclusive Elvisly Yours collection; Sally & Richard Greenhill for pages 16-17 (bottom) and 118-119; Gruppo Editoriale Fabbri for page 16 (middle left); Hewett Street Studios for page 13 (top); Mieke Maas/Image Bank for page 77 (bottom left); Chris Moyse for pages 4, 5, 6 (top left), 6 (top middle), 9, 12, 18, 31, 36 (left), 36-37 (top), 47, 48, 56, 58 (top right), 58 (bottom left), 58 (lower middle right), 58 (bottom right), 59, 64, 66, 74 (top left), 82, 84 (left), 84-85, 110 and 111; The Photographers' Library for page 68 (top); Pictor International-London for pages 52, 74 (top middle), 74 (top right) and 74 (bottom middle); Picturepoint-London for pages 8 (top right), 16 (bottom middle), 32 (right) and 88; Rex Features Ltd. for page 68 (bottom); Royal Society for the Prevention of Accidents for pages 67 (top) and 67 (middle bottom); Sporting Pictures (UK) Ltd. for page 24; Stockphotos International for page 77 (bottom right); Susan Griggs Agency Ltd. for pages 21 (top) and 78; Syndication International Ltd. for page 26; Tony Stone Photo Library-London for page 69 (middle left) and for permission to reproduce the illustration on page 96-97, from a copyright photograph; Zefa Picture Library (UK) Ltd. for page 74 (bottom right).

We have been unable to trace the copyright holder of the photograph on page 83, and would be grateful for any information that would enable us to do so.

All photographs not listed above were taken by the Longman Photographic Unit.

Our special thanks to the following for their help during location photography:
Alan Ewington, Harlow; Harlow Theatre Trust Ltd./The Playhouse, Harlow; Harveys Ltd., Harlow; Herts & Essex General Hospital, Bishop's Stortford; J..Wasson fruiterer & greengrocer, Old Harlow; Martins Newsagents PLC., Old Harlow; METWEST Ltd. dispensing chemist, Harlow; Travellers Fair, London NW1.

Illustrated by Paw Print, Terry McKivragen, Art Brigade, Clive Spong, Mulkern Rutherford Technical Illustrations, Liz Hankins, Haro, Oena Armstrong, Ian Flemming (Sally Launder).

Designed by John Strange, assisted by David Foster.

For teachers in Spain:
Autorizado por el Ministerio de Educación y Ciencia con fecha 1.12.83 (B.O.E. 17.1.84).